Valerie Knowles

Valerie Knowles was born in Montreal and has a B.A. (Honours History) from Smith College and an M.A. (History) from McGill University. In addition to writing for newspapers, magazines, and federal government departments, she has taught history and worked as an archivist. She has published several non-fiction works, including *From Telegrapher to Titan: The Life of William C. Van Horne*, which won the 2004 University of British Columbia Medal for Canadian Biography and the 2005 City of Ottawa Book Award for Non-Fiction. Valerie lives in Ottawa.

In the same collection

Ven Begamudré, *Isaac Brock: Larger Than Life*
Lynne Bowen, *Robert Dunsmuir: Laird of the Mines*
Kate Braid, *Emily Carr: Rebel Artist*
Kathryn Bridge, *Phyllis Munday: Mountaineer*
Edward Butts, *Henry Hudson: New World Voyager*
William Chalmers, *George Mercer Dawson: Geologist, Scientist, Explorer*
Anne Cimon, *Susanna Moodie: Pioneer Author*
Deborah Cowley, *Lucille Teasdale: Doctor of Courage*
Gary Evans, *John Grierson: Trailblazer of Documentary Film*
Julie H. Ferguson, *James Douglas: Father of British Columbia*
Judith Fitzgerald, *Marshall McLuhan: Wise Guy*
lian goodall, *William Lyon Mackenzie King: Dreams and Shadows*
Tom Henighan, *Vilhjalmur Stefansson: Arctic Adventurer*
Stephen Eaton Hume, *Frederick Banting: Hero, Healer, Artist*
Naïm Kattan, *A.M. Klein: Poet and Prophet*
Betty Keller, *Pauline Johnson: First Aboriginal Voice of Canada*
Heather Kirk, *Mazo de la Roche: Rich and Famous Writer*
Vladimir Konieczny, *Glenn Gould: A Musical Force*
Michelle Labrèche-Larouche, *Emma Albani: International Star*
Wayne Larsen, *A.Y. Jackson: A Love for the Land*
Wayne Larsen, *James Wilson Morrice: Painter of Light and Shadow*
Francine Legaré, *Samuel de Champlain: Father of New France*
Margaret Macpherson, *Nellie McClung: Voice for the Voiceless*
Nicholas Maes, *Robertson Davies: Magician of Words*
Dave Margoshes, *Tommy Douglas: Building the New Society*
Marguerite Paulin, *René Lévesque: Charismatic Leader*
Raymond Plante, *Jacques Plante: Behind the Mask*
Jim Poling Sr., *Tecumseh: Shooting Star, Crouching Panther*
T.F. Rigelhof, *George Grant: Redefining Canada*
Tom Shardlow, *David Thompson: A Trail by Stars*
Arthur Slade, *John Diefenbaker: An Appointment with Destiny*
Roderick Stewart, *Wilfrid Laurier: A Pledge for Canada*
Sharon Stewart, *Louis Riel: Firebrand*
André Vanasse, *Gabrielle Roy: A Passion for Writing*
John Wilson, *John Franklin: Traveller on Undiscovered Seas*
John Wilson, *Norman Bethune: A Life of Passionate Conviction*
Rachel Wyatt, *Agnes Macphail: Champion of the Underdog*

A QUEST BIOGRAPHY

WILLIAM C. VAN HORNE

RAILWAY TITAN

VALERIE KNOWLES

DUNDURN PRESS
TORONTO

Copy Editor: Jennifer McKnight
Design: Jennifer Scott
Printer: Marquis

Library and Archives Canada Cataloguing in Publication

Knowles, Valerie
William C. Van Horne : railway titan / Valerie Knowles.

Includes bibliographical references and index.
ISBN 978-1-55488-702-6

1. Van Horne, William Cornelius, Sir, 1843-1915. 2. Canadian Pacific Railway Company--Presidents--Biography. 3. Capitalists and financiers--Canada--Biography. I. Title.

HE2808.2.V3K59 2010 971.05092 C2009-907443-5

1 2 3 4 5 14 13 12 11 10

We acknowledge the support of the **Canada Council for the Arts** and the **Ontario Arts Council** for our publishing program. We also acknowledge the financial support of the **Government of Canada** through the **Canada Book Fund** and **The Association for the Export of Canadian Books**, and the **Government of Ontario** through the **Ontario Book Publishers Tax Credit program**, and the **Ontario Media Development Corporation**.

Care has been taken to trace the ownership of copyright material used in this book. The author and the publisher welcome any information enabling them to rectify any references or credits in subsequent editions.

J. Kirk Howard, President

Printed and bound in Canada.
www.dundurn.com

Dundurn Press
3 Church Street, Suite 500
Toronto, Ontario, Canada
M5E 1M2

Gazelle Book Services Limited
White Cross Mills
High Town, Lancaster, England
LA1 4XS

Dundurn Press
2250 Military Road
Tonawanda, NY
U.S.A. 14150

Contents

Acknowledgements

To Rosemary Shipton, who did the substantive editing of this book, I owe my deepest thanks. She did a magnificent job of tightening my prose and posing insightful questions that demanded answers. I also extend my thanks to Jennifer McKnight, who did the copy-editing and piloted the manuscript through to completion.

1

The Man Who Built the Trans-Canada Railway

At last the development that William Cornelius Van Horne has set his sights on has arrived: the driving of the last spike on the Canadian Pacific Railway's trans-Canada line. It is November 7, 1885, a dull, raw day in Craigellachie in British Columbia's Eagle Pass, west of Revelstoke in the Rocky Mountains.

The photograph that records this epochal event in Canadian history shows a phalanx of dark fir trees and cedars and in front of it a crowd of men. Workmen, surveyors, construction managers, and curious onlookers, they crane forward to watch a white-bearded figure in a stovepipe hat stoop to pick up his maul and complete the line. The first choice to perform the task was Governor General Lord Lansdowne, the son-in-law of Queen Victoria, but neither he nor George Stephen, the CPR president, can be here. So the honour falls to Donald Smith, a company director who twelve years later will become Lord Strathcona.

Smith swings at the tie held in place by Major A.B. Rogers, the engineer in charge of the CPR's Mountain Division, but his first blow bends the iron spike so badly that it is quickly replaced with another. On his second attempt Smith succeeds. The audience, overawed, remains silent for a moment, then breaks out with a resounding cheer. Before long, the shrill whistles of the surrounding locomotives join in the hearty applause.

William Van Horne, the CPR vice-president, the man who had managed the building of this ribbon of steel that linked the country east to west, steps forward to make his speech: "All I can say," he says tersely, "is that the work has been well done in every way."

He has succeeded in hurling twenty-four hundred miles of railway track across half a continent, much of it in wilderness. Moreover, he has done so in far less time than anyone had predicted. Alexander Mackenzie, Canada's second prime minster, announced in October 1875 that the road "could not likely be completed in ten years with all the power of men and all the money of the Empire." The current Canadian government also allowed a decade for the construction of the railway, but Van Horne has managed to complete it in less than half that time — four and a half years.

The superhuman dynamo who pushed through the construction of the Canadian Pacific's main line was an American. William Cornelius Van Horne, the son of Cornelius and Mary Van Horne, was born on February 3, 1843, in the now abandoned village of Chelsea, just west of the town of Frankfort in Illinois.

He was descended from Jan Cornelissen Van Horne, a true pioneer who left Amsterdam for America in 1635 and helped to found New Amsterdam (now New York City) on Manhattan Island. Van

Courtesy of the Notman Photographic Archives, McCord Museum of Canadian History, Montreal, MP-000.25.971.

Perhaps the most famous Canadian photo. It shows Lord Strathcona driving the last spike at Craigellachie. The bearded, corpulent figure on his right is Van Horne.

Horne's paternal grandfather, Abram, or "the Dominie," as he was affectionately known, was a highly respected minister in the Dutch Reformed Church. He followed the example of other Van Horne males by marrying into a prominent Dutch-American family, the Covenhoven clan. Although Abram's ministry covered a large area in New York State and his fees were lamentably small, he was able to maintain himself, his wife, and nine children in comfort thanks to the substantial legacies that both he and his wife had received from their fathers. With this generous assistance, they supported as many as twenty slaves and continued the Van Horne and Covenhoven family traditions of abundant hospitality.

Van Horne's father was therefore born into a stable and prosperous family. The Dominie hoped that Cornelius would also enter the ministry, but this high-spirited son had other plans. In 1813, when he was only nineteen, he married Elizabeth Vedder and the following year, after graduating from Union College in New York, he embarked on law studies. Cornelius was enjoying the income and prestige from a successful law practice when, in 1832, he suddenly uprooted his family and took them by covered wagon to the distant frontier state of Illinois. Like thousands of other restless Yankees at the time, he turned his back on the sophisticated community in which he had grown up and the relative security that it offered and struck out for the American Midwest. What motivated him, we do not know. It might have been a sense of adventure or a wish to escape the conventions of life on the eastern seaboard. Or it might have been some vague, undefined dissatisfaction and a belief that utopia existed in the wilderness of Illinois, destined to become the fastest-growing territory in the world in the mid-nineteenth century.

In today's world of paved roads and sleek airplanes and trains, it is hard to imagine the gruelling journey that the young family took. For transportation, they relied on the "prairie schooner," a heavily laden, covered wagon that bumped along dusty, bone-bruising trails. To reach their destination, the Van Hornes travelled for hundreds of miles along these rutted paths, forded rivers, and braved severe weather conditions. As they did so, they hoped to avoid the many deadly diseases common at the time or confrontations with hostile Indians.

Once arrived in Illinois, the family cleared land and constructed a cabin in New Lenox Township, in the northern part of the state. Two years later, however, they moved to nearby Frankfort, settling about a mile west of the hamlet, where Van Horne was born. Their new home was carved out of the wilderness on land that would be surveyed for the town of Chelsea in 1848–49.

In this sparsely settled part of what would become Will County, Van Horne's father became a respected community leader. He continued his law practice and also served as the first schoolmaster in the area and as Will County's first postmaster and justice of the peace. In all these roles, he was respected for his force of character, his shrewdness, and his "bold, outspoken way of giving vent to his honest convictions." In due course his son William came to be noted for these same characteristics.

Unfortunately, Cornelius's early years in Illinois were scarred by tragedy. A daughter died in infancy and, in 1838, his wife, Elizabeth, passed away, leaving him with four young children. He sent them to live with relatives or friends. To add to his burden, in the winter of 1839–40 the family home was "consumed by fire."

After the blaze, which claimed his homestead, barns, books, and other personal effects, Cornelius set about building a new home. In this he was aided by his brother Matthew, a prosperous farmer who had settled nearby with another brother. It was to this log house in 1842 that Cornelius brought his second wife, Mary Minier Richards, the daughter of a Pennsylvanian mother of French origin and an American father of German descent who had immigrated to the colonies as a young man.

William Cornelius Van Horne was the first child of this second marriage and, in less than a decade, he was joined by four siblings: Augustus Charles in 1844, Elizabeth in 1846, Theodore in 1848, and Mary in 1852. Interestingly, both of William's brothers also took up a railway career, but neither rose to such lofty heights as he did. As the first-born, William soon exhibited many of the characteristics that psychologists associate with the oldest child — natural leadership, reliability, conscientiousness, and a striving for perfection. These same traits would prove indispensable in advancing Van Horne's career.

For a person whose destiny was to be linked with railways, the 1840s was an exciting period in which to be born in the United States. In the first explosion of railway construction, the amount of track more than tripled, from three to nine thousand miles. In the 1850s, work gangs laid another twenty-one thousand miles of track and provided the country east of the Mississippi River with its basic overland transportation networks. The 1840s also witnessed the perfection of railway construction techniques and the tentative emergence of the railway as the "first modern business." Such was the enormity of the impact of these developments that we can compare it to the influence of the Internet on present-day North American business and society.

This decade also saw the emergence of the second marvel of communication — the telegraph — which also had a profound influence on Van Horne's life. In 1843, Congress voted to pay Samuel Morse to build the first telegraph line in the United States, from Washington to Baltimore. The following year Morse sent the first message on this line. Soon the telegraph was sending instantaneous messages along copper wires, which ran alongside the railway lines that would shortly span the American continent. Like the railway, the telegraph would help to shrink distance and create a sense of community. It would also further the railway careers of those who, like Van Horne, became knowledgeable about its technology and adept at using it.

Before the family moved to Joliet, Illinois, some fourteen miles from Chelsea, William Van Horne's world was defined by the homestead and its immediate surroundings. Most important was the spacious log house built on the brow of a hill overlooking a valley. In the woods, not far from the house, was a stable and other log outbuildings, while nestled in the valley, beside Hickory Creek, was a largely inactive sawmill.

When he was six years old, young William began attending school. Weather permitting, he would trudge a couple of miles to the small schoolhouse, undoubtedly a one-room building, where children of all ages were taught by a single teacher in a room heated by a wood-burning stove. To reach this Spartan place of instruction, he made his way through woods, hoping all the while that he would not encounter one of the wolves that also made its home there.

These rambles sowed the seeds for two hobbies that would become lifelong passions — paleontology and art. He had few toys to play with, so he began to collect pebbles from the stream that flowed at the base of the hill near his home. One day, when he was still very young, he found a thin piece of shiny black stone. He eagerly scooped it up, but, to his great disappointment, it changed to a lacklustre grey as it dried. Still, he carried it home to his resourceful mother, hoping she would be able to restore its bright colour. She could not, but she did something even better.

She told William that his stone was a piece of slate and that he could use it to make marks on another piece of slate. Intrigued, he began to scratch on slate at every opportunity and soon moved on to crude drawings of children, dogs, and horses. When the soft slate wore out and he could not find any more pieces to replace it, he turned to drawing on the white-washed walls of the family home. Mary, who also had a gift for art, encouraged him to continue, and Cornelius aided and abetted the cause by bringing home chalks and pencils from Joliet. Before long, young William had covered every wall in the house, as high as his small arm could reach, with drawings. His parents had opened a new world of art to him, and, in time, he became a proficient amateur artist.

When William was seven, his parents took him with them on one of their visits to Joliet, a small town some thirty-seven miles southwest of Chicago and named after the French-Canadian explorer Louis Joliet. It was William's first trip outside the valley, and he never forgot how awestruck he was by the number of two-storey houses he found in the town. The following year, 1851, Cornelius moved the whole family to Joliet, no doubt to obtain better schooling for his children and more opportunities for himself. All at once, young William's horizons expanded dramatically.

Joliet, a flourishing town of some two thousand inhabitants, seemed huge and impressive to the young boy. It had a school, a church, a courthouse, shops, and also the National Hotel, with such wonders as fresh spring water in its basement kitchen and a bell system connecting the rooms to the office. Ever since the opening of the Illinois-Michigan canal in 1848, this landmark hostelry had provided accommodation for the thousands of passengers who travelled by boat along those waters. And, when the Chicago, Rock Island, and Pacific Railroad came to Joliet in 1852, the hotel began shuttling passengers from its front door to the station in a bright yellow bus drawn by a team of grey horses.

No sooner had Cornelius Van Horne resumed his law practice and settled the family into their new home than he plunged into municipal politics. In 1852 Joliet was incorporated as a city and, in its first municipal election, Cornelius was elected mayor. As he also served as justice of the peace for Joliet and Will County, he had considerable status in the community.

William revelled in the new opportunities he found in Joliet for collecting rocks and in his free time eagerly explored the grasslands along the banks of the Des Plaines River. He noticed that some of the rocks contained fossils, so added a separate category in his collection for them. One day he found a perfect trilobite outline embedded in a stone on Joliet's main street, and he returned that night with a hammer to chip it out. So began his hobby of collecting fossils, and, in the course of his life, he would discover and classify many new species. Like so many other Victorians, he became a zealous naturalist, keen not only to build up his collections but to organize them, too.

In his later years, William Van Horne became convinced that every boy should have a hobby that involved a collection of some sort. There was no better way to prepare the mind for complex management, he wrote to a friend:

> The best thing a boy can do is to begin to collect. Let him collect something — I don't care what it is — and you will find he begins to notice, and from noticing, he begins to classify and arrange. Interest develops, and wherever he goes there is nothing connected with his collection about which he is not keenly interested. The real education for a boy is simply a matter of impressions. These cannot be selected for him, but they colour the whole of his life.

The school that William attended in Joliet was typical of its time: it drilled him in the "Three Rs" — reading, writing, and arithmetic — but covered little more. Nevertheless, despite the dull routine and strict discipline, he mastered the basic skills well. He also became an avid reader, grabbing every book he could lay his hands on and soaking up knowledge like a sponge.

Young William's love of books even caused him to switch Sunday schools. He and his brother Augustus initially went to the one at the church their mother attended, St. John's Universalist Church. When William heard that the Methodist Sunday school had "the better books," he persuaded his parents to let him go there. And so he was exposed to the teachings of Methodism, whose emphasis on self-denial, personal holiness, and careful stewardship helped to inspire the lives of many well-known capitalists, such as Sir Joseph Flavelle, one of Canada's most respected businessmen and philanthropists in the late nineteenth and early twentieth centuries. If these qualities helped Flavelle in his meteoric rise from humble beginnings to celebrated businessman and financier, they probably influenced William, too — even though he had no interest in organized religion as an adult.

William's world was suddenly shattered in July 1854, when he was only eleven: his father came down with cholera and died. Although he left no description of how his father's death affected him personally, this loss must have been profound. It was probably responsible for the bouts of melancholy that afflicted him in the years just before his marriage. Cornelius Van Horne left a good name, but, his son did say, he also left "a lot of accounts payable and some bad accounts receivable." As a lawyer, he seldom took fees, and, even when he possessed not a penny himself, he often refused payment for his services. In a draft letter written to his grandson decades later, William Van Horne confessed, "I could not understand it then, and I am not quite sure that I do now, but this occurred in a newly settled country where all were poor alike."

Mary was left with five children to raise and, ever resourceful and courageous, she managed to keep "bread," usually hominy, on the table by taking in sewing and by selling produce from her garden. Even so, the family was forced to move from a comfortable home with spacious grounds to a small cottage. While still a child, William learned that life is a struggle and that his progress through it would depend to a great extent on his own efforts.

To help support his family, William worked whenever he could out of school hours, splitting logs and delivering telegraph messages from Joliet's telegraph operators. While waiting for the messages, he listened carefully to the tapping instrument and watched the tape slowly unwind as it spelled out the message in dashes and dots. Later he wrote: "I was put on the station service and as I was very young, the men didn't mind my asking questions, and what is more, they answered them and told me things." He learned more than anyone realized at the time, and it is quite probable that this new technology subtly but effectively gave him a sense of the larger world beyond Joliet.

Despite his intelligence and superb memory, William was easily bored at school. To fill the hours, he often drew caricatures of his teachers and the students sitting near him. In the schoolyard he enjoyed brawling with the other boys, offered to take on all comers, and usually won. But all these boisterous hijinks came to an end the day he was caught caricaturing the school principal. The punishment he received was so severe that, although he was only thirteen, he chose never to return to school. By then, however, he had acquired quite a good education by the minimal standards of the day. He could read, write, and reason well. More important, he was curious about many things and he loved to learn. These qualities served him well as he left his boyhood behind and entered the adult world of work and responsibility.

2

Early Career

Once he dropped out of school, William Van Horne began to study telegraphy seriously at the city office. He knew that he now had to master a trade that would provide him with full-time employment. Perhaps he also realized that this method of communication would open career doors for him. Certainly he impressed the adults he met. One of those who recognized the potential in the precocious but still slight, young teenager was a railway man who observed in a letter:

> My dear young friend, yours of a few days since came duly to hand and we were glad to hear from you and that you are doing so well.... You are young now and by proper conduct can grow up to be a good man, if not a great one. Your destiny mostly lies in your own hands.

> What you will at your age by perseverance and determination you can greatly accomplish. So aim high. What is this life without accomplishing some great good, which altho you do not directly see it extends far and wide. Have some grand and glorious object in view and not live as some live to eat drink and sleep.

A few months later, when Van Horne was fourteen, the Joliet telegraph operator found employment for him as a telegrapher with the celebrated Illinois Central Railroad Company. Founded in 1851, it had already completed seven hundred miles of track to make it the single longest railway in the world. In the years to come, it would play an important role in converting much of unoccupied Illinois into a settled, prosperous area.

Van Horne enjoyed his new job in the mechanical superintendent's office, located in Chicago, but he did not last long in the position. Once again, his love of practical jokes proved his downfall. One day, he ran a ground wire from a storage battery to a steel plate in the rail yard. Then he amused himself by watching the contortions of the yardmen who stepped on it. Unfortunately, the local superintendent also trod on the wire and, being knowledgeable about the principles of electricity, quickly realized what was up. In no time at all he was in the perpetrator's office, where Van Horne promptly confessed that he was the culprit. The superintendent fired him on the spot. With this sudden dismissal, the teenager returned to his mother's cottage in Joliet, a chastened and more mature young man.

Fortunately, one of his good friends, Henry Knowlton, was the son of the assistant superintendent of the Cut Off, a forty-five-mile-long line that ran from Joliet to Lake Junction, Indiana, and was operated by the Michigan Central Railroad. Through this connection, Van Horne was soon able to obtain employment as a messenger and freight checker for the company. In his new job he frequently came into contact with local businessmen, whom he invariably impressed with his industriousness and shrewd intelligence. Captain Ellwood was one such man and, years later, in 1916, he recalled: "I remember him in 1854, a thoughtful little fellow, so frail that I thought he would never be strong. But when I came back from the military academy in France a few years later he astonished me. He looked stronger — healthy even, and he was already being talked about in Joliet as an unusual young fellow."

After holding his new position for only a few months, Van Horne convinced his boss that the Cut Off should have an independent telegraph line and that he should operate it. The line was duly installed, and the teenager immersed himself in his duties as a telegrapher. With constant access to the telegraph, Van Horne was able to perfect his skills to the point where he could decipher incoming messages merely by listening to the instrument's clicks and clacks and had no need to "read" the tape. He became famous as the first operator in his district, and one of the first in the country, to master this feat. And while he was chalking up these distinctions, the new technology was taking him far beyond the boundaries of his town and introducing him to a wider world.

Van Horne's duties as a telegrapher did not claim all his attention. He was already familiar with the storehouse, but now he set out to learn how other operations on the Cut Off worked. Ever the inquisitive youngster, he began to make drawings of illustrations in the draughtsman's books during his lunch hour and at night to understudy the duties of the accountant, the cashier, the timekeeper, and the other men around him. He did so while deliberately cultivating his already remarkable memory. Whenever he had a moment he would challenge those around him to contests in which they all tried to memorize the numbers on the cars of long trains that passed through the yard. Van Horne was usually the winner.

Up to this point, Van Horne's boundless energy and ambition seemed to be unfocused; he just wanted to learn as many railroading skills as he could. When he was eighteen, though, he decided on a particular goal — to run a railway. The trigger was a visit the general superintendent (the chief executive) of the Michigan Central Railroad made to the Cut Off one day. His opulent private car and the ceremony surrounding his arrival made such a forceful impression on Van Horne that he decided on the spot that he wanted that job.

Having promised himself that he would manage a railway system rather than create one, Van Horne set out with single-minded determination to meet his goal, convinced that "he who makes an ambitious time-table is likely to run by it." He thought that a general superintendent must surely know everything about a railway, so he gave up all the holiday time that was owed to him and worked weeknights and Sundays to inform himself about the details of every department.

These were certainly propitious years in which to launch a railway career, as railways were expanding rapidly. In fact, by 1860 the United States had a larger rail network than all the existing networks in the rest of the world combined. The most spectacular growth occurred in Van Horne's part of the continent, the old Northwest, where railway mileage had increased about eightfold during the previous decade. While the railway revolution was making itself felt, the telegraph was shrinking the world with its fast, regular, and dependable means of communication. Both of these marvels would profoundly alter American life, but none more so than the railway. Belching smoke from their large funnel-shaped chimneys and showering sparks, steam locomotives roared through the countryside, knitting cities and towns closer together, opening up wilderness areas, and providing the transportation so essential to high-volume agricultural and industrial production.

Although Van Horne was dedicated to his job and his advancement, he still found time to pursue his interest in paleontology — an area of study that, like railway management, makes extensive use of categorization. In addition to reading widely on the subject, Van Horne, sometimes accompanied by a few of his friends, tramped the countryside around Joliet and even further afield in search of new specimens. His collection would eventually boast nine previously unclassified specimens — they were named after him and have the descriptive suffix *Van Hornei* in paleontological encyclopedias.

Inspired by the establishment of the Illinois Natural History Society at Bloomington, Illinois, Van Horne and his comrades founded the Agassiz Club of Joliet in 1859, named after Jean Louis Agassiz, a famous geologist, naturalist, and teacher. Members were expected to go on weekend trips to places as far distant as twenty-five miles away. When not scavenging the countryside for new fossils, Van Horne and his pals carried on an extensive correspondence with geology authorities and arranged their collections, carefully observing the Smithsonian Institution's directions for the care and preservation of specimens. But Van Horne was the only real leader of the group: once he moved away from Joliet, the club dissolved, and with it his dream of establishing a local museum. Decades later, however, his own fossil collection would be given to the University of Chicago.

Van Horne was working as a telegrapher in the dingy Cut Off office when the American Civil War broke out in the spring of 1861. Before this bitter conflict ended four years later, it would devastate a third of the country, claim more than six hundred thousand lives, and hopelessly maim thousands of others in body or mind. In the early days of the war, however, it would never have occurred to most Americans, including Van Horne, that the conflict would turn the entire country into "one vast central hospital," as Walt Whitman, America's renowned poet, described the war's impact. Like so many young people of his day, the combative Van Horne was stirred by tales of battle. Even late in life he argued that universal peace was neither "possible nor desirable" and that "all the manliness of the civilized world is due to wars or the need of being prepared for wars."

Illinois and the other free states were gripped by a groundswell of patriotic fever when the Confederate flag was raised over Fort Sumter, South Carolina, on April 14, 1861. Predictably, when news of the fort's surrender reached Joliet, its citizens acted with shock and outrage. An old fairground was quickly converted into a camp, and by mid-May it boasted a full regiment, including two companies from Will County. Almost four thousand men from that county alone volunteered for service in the war, and more than five hundred of them would die in battle, from wounds or disease, or during internment in prison camps.

Among those eager to assist the Union cause was eighteen-year-old William Van Horne. One morning, without consulting anyone in the Cut Off office, he enlisted for service in the federal army. As soon as the news reached his work place, however, the assistant superintendent interceded to have his registration cancelled. He was determined that Van Horne would remain on the job: not only was he the principal support of his widowed mother but, as an exceptionally capable telegrapher, his services were indispensable to the Cut Off office.

Despite this praise, Van Horne became alarmed early in the war when rumours began to circulate that the declining traffic and drop in earnings caused by the conflict would force the Michigan Central to lay off some of its workers. But when Van Horne's boss realized that the office was fast becoming an important centre for troop transportation, he decided that his telegrapher was an essential staff member. The young man was so relieved to keep his job that, when the assistant superintendent asked him how much additional work he could take on, he promptly replied that he could do any task at all. He immediately set out to prove himself: drawing on his ample store of initiative and knowledge of the office, the shops, and the yards, he quickly became the assistant superintendent's right-hand man.

His new responsibilities should have kept Van Horne more than fully occupied, but they did not. He still needed outlets for his surplus energy and inventiveness, and every so often he played practical jokes on his work mates or even the townspeople. Unfortunately, some of them were in bad taste. On one occasion he sent an authentic-sounding telegram announcing a great Union victory on the battlefield. When the excited citizens heard the news, they hastened to run up flags and celebrate. The festivities ended abruptly once the Chicago newspapers arrived and the war-weary residents realized that they had been duped. An angry party went in search of Van Horne at the Cut Off office, only to discover that he had wisely headed for home.

Van Horne climbed another step up the railway ladder in 1862, when he accepted an offer from the Chicago and Alton

Railroad to become its telegraph operator and ticket agent at Joliet. The substantial increase in salary that came with the job reflected just how demanding his duties and responsibilities were. This was especially true of the telegrapher's job, which required an even-tempered individual with superior organizational skills and the ability to cooperate and work effectively with a whole team of people.

In this new position, Van Horne quickly demonstrated his resourcefulness. He noticed that butter deteriorated when it was left in a warm storage shed while awaiting shipment, so he arranged for it to be stored in a primitive cold-storage chamber he designed. He reasoned that if cold temperatures preserved the quality of the butter, farmers would obtain higher prices for their product and ship more of it by the Chicago and Alton, thereby increasing the railway's earnings. His resourcefulness and foresight paid off — and the company quickly introduced his invention at other freight sheds on the line.

Two years later, in 1864, Van Horne was promoted to train dispatcher at Bloomington, a Chicago and Alton divisional point located in a rich agricultural area in central Illinois some ninety miles southwest of Joliet. This new position represented a considerable advance in his railway career, as it paid much better than the one he had held at Joliet. The Civil War was still raging, and trains were busy hauling troops, foodstuffs, horses, forage, ordinance, lumber, equipment, and supplies southward and returning soldiers and prisoners northward. Van Horne was therefore kept extremely busy helping to direct the flow of people and supplies from Chicago to St. Louis on the one main line then operated by the Chicago and Alton. Some twenty years later, during the North-West Rebellion of 1885 in Canada, he drew on the valuable experience he had acquired during this earlier wartime period.

In the early days on the railways, before messages could be sent by telegraph, train schedules and other orders were communicated verbally by the managers and then memorized by the crews. The system worked reasonably well so long as everything went as planned. When a train could not keep to its assigned schedule because of mechanical failure, a shortage of fuel, track damage, or some other unexpected development, however, no one except those operating the train knew exactly where it was on the line. Once the telegraph became a common communication tool in the 1860s, a dispatcher could establish the location of any train in his jurisdiction at all times. Skilled telegraphers like Van Horne were therefore much in demand.

Van Horne's exceptional abilities led his superiors to assign him the night shift, normally worked by only the most competent dispatchers. Between 6:30 p.m. and 5:00 a.m., he watched and directed the movement of up to twenty trains at any one time on almost three hundred miles of track. When all the trains were "on time," there was little, if anything, to do; but when one or more of them fell behind schedule, he had to plot new locations and times for trains running at different speeds, or in opposite directions, or both. It was exacting, complicated work that he likened to playing a game of chess, though not nearly so fascinating. Still, he was quick to agree that a single error in dispatching could pose a serious threat to life and property, or both, and result in an abrupt end to a dispatcher's career.

Van Horne had a lot going for him by now: an impressive expertise in telegraphy and train dispatching, plus a wide knowledge of the workings of other train departments. These skills, together with his personal magnetism and wit, helped to make him a recognized leader on the railway. Whenever disputes arose involving the interpretation of train rules and other related matters, he was always asked for his opinion. Such respect, of course, fed his self-confidence and made him feel at ease in his relationships with his superiors.

One day he was in the room as the Chicago and Alton's general superintendent devised a new railway schedule: the system back then was to arrange strings and pins on charts to indicate where trains should run and cross paths. When he could no longer contain his impatience with this laborious display, Van Horne muttered, "That's a hell of a way to make a time-sheet." Getting to his feet, the superintendent replied, "If you can do it better, take the job." Van Horne immediately took over — with excellent results — and the arrangement of train schedules was thereafter assigned to him.

When Van Horne moved to Bloomington it was a mere prairie town, noted for its railway shops and its corn, but not for its civic amenities. For a young man who loved to visit Chicago's museums and art galleries and who delighted in attractive surroundings, Bloomington was a most unlovely place: a blue-collar town with a smoke-belching powerhouse and an abundance of grime. It is no wonder that he described it as "outside the limits of civilization." Perhaps even more distressing, his home was a rented room located in a working class section. In these circumstances, he turned to watercolour painting in his few leisure hours and indulged his interest in science. The demands of his job allowed him little time for fossil hunting, although he did manage a few thirty-five-mile treks in search of new specimens.

Even more important, he developed a friendship with the multitalented John Wesley Powell, a professor of geology and curator of the museum at Illinois Wesleyan University in Bloomington. Powell, who became noted for his pioneering classification of North American Indian languages and his survey of the Rocky Mountain region, was probably responsible for putting Van Horne in touch with his idol from Joliet days, Louis Agassiz. When he heard that the great man would be passing through Bloomington on a particular train, Van Horne met it, introduced himself, and travelled with the celebrity for some distance. Their conversation culminated in a correspondence that lasted until Agassiz's death in 1873.

Geology was not the only science that got Van Horne's attention. He also pursued an interest in chemistry and botany, sometimes setting aside a Sunday to "review his chemistry lessons." Astronomy was another field that intrigued him, so much so that he drew up elaborate charts to follow the progress of a comet sighted in Bloomington on April 16, 1868.

By now, though, the greatest personal interest in Van Horne's life was not art or science, but an attractive and well-educated young woman, Lucy Adaline Hurd.

Van Horne was still based in Joliet when he met the young woman, affectionately known as Addie or Adda, who would become his devoted wife. Born in 1837 into a middle-class family that revered education and placed ideals before material possessions, she had studied music, taught Sunday school in the Universalist Church of America, and cultivated an interest in literature. What really set her apart from the other young women of her era, however, was her education. When she was nineteen, she had graduated with a B.A. from Lombard College, a liberal institution founded by members of the Universalist Church and located in Galesburg, Illinois — her birth place. Addie Hurd was six years older than Van Horne, and she undoubtedly took some pains to hide it.

When Adaline's father Erastus, a civil engineer, died in 1857, the family was plunged into poverty. To satisfy creditors and make ends meet, they sold much of their property and Addie went to work as a music teacher. Family lore has it that the young couple first met in the early 1860s in Joliet, where Adaline and her widowed mother were living. Their chance meeting occurred at the train station, where Addie was stranded without a ride home after her train arrived late from Chicago. Although William was normally very shy in the presence of women, he gallantly offered to escort her home. They set off, but not before he shoved the pipe he was smoking into his jacket pocket. As he walked on, absorbed in conversation, he suddenly detected the smell of burning wool. He then remembered that his pipe was still alight and quickly smothered the embers as best he could.

It was probably Adaline's refined beauty that made the most forceful impression on Van Horne that day. If he considered her beautiful, he was not alone. His friends were completely smitten by her looks. A future clergyman, the Reverend E.P. Savage, confessed that when he and some other friends heard that Van Horne was to marry Miss Hurd, "It just took our breath away. All the rest of the boys in the Agassiz Club liked parties and girls except Will. And here he was engaged to the most beautiful girl we knew." Van Horne was probably also captivated by Addie's dignity and reserve — two qualities that were later remarked on by others. The well-known British journalist and diarist Henry Beckles Willson, for instance, described her as "a quiet, intelligent woman, of simple manners and entirely devoted to her husband and family."

By the fall of 1864, when the South was being pummelled by Union forces, the couple were exchanging letters, as William had by then moved to Bloomington. Two years later, the friendship had blossomed into a true love affair that saw him shuttling back and forth by passenger or freight train between Bloomington and Joliet. When they were apart, as happened most of the time, he took every opportunity to write to her, frequently filling his letters with affectionate concern for her well-being. "You must be very careful, dearest, and not in any way endanger your health," he advised on her forthcoming trip to Vermont to visit relatives. "I fear you are not sufficiently cautious in that respect.... And in travelling you must not hesitate to call upon the conductors for any information or assistance that may be conducive to your safety and comfort."

In his longing to be with Adaline, William convinced himself that only marriage would put a permanent end to the "aimless, cold, loveless and mechanical existence" of his life without her. He hoped that he and Addie would marry in the fall of 1866, but for some reason the ceremony did not take place that autumn. Clearly Addie was in love with the taciturn young man who, despite occasional spells of melancholy, seemed headed for great things. "I thought of you constantly & was only happy in closing my eyes & transporting myself to the time when I could again be with you & relive the only true pleasure which your presence alone can give," she wrote to him in the summer of 1866.

Despite this love for her fiancé, Addie was apprehensive about marriage. Her "insecure health," as she ambiguously expressed it, seems to explain some of this hesitation. Her mother's unflattering view of marriage probably also played a role. Moreover, because Addie had her own career outside the home, she may also have harboured some reservations about relinquishing her independence. Whatever the explanation, the delay caused William considerable suspense and anxiety. Finally, on a cold, wet, March 26, 1867, they married in Christ Church in

Joliet — the day after William obtained a marriage licence and, perhaps significantly, while Addie's mother was away in Vermont visiting her relations.

Shortly after the marriage, Addie's mother, Anna, as well as William's mother, Mary, and his unmarried sister, Mary, moved to Bloomington to share a large rented home that Van Horne had repapered, whitewashed, and painted. This was a highly unusual arrangement, even for Victorian times, but, fortunately, the extended family got on well together. With all these women to minister to his needs, Van Horne could look forward to enjoying a warm, serene home environment — something he craved. Although he realized that his life would be buffeted from time to time by adversity, he knew that he could always look to his home for comfort and solace from the pressures of a job with irregular hours and frequent changes of residence. This assurance would prove extremely important to him as he continued his steady progress up the railway hierarchy.

Mrs. William Van Horne in 1889. The Canadian novelist William A. Fraser described her as "the most gracious woman I ever met in my life."

Courtesy of the Notman Photographic Archives, McCord Museum of Canadian History, Montreal, 11-89974.

Meanwhile, he had friendships and leisure pursuits to cultivate in Bloomington, a far more appealing place now that he had his own home and family there. Along with the well-known professor of natural history, chemistry, and botany, Dr. J.A. Sewall, he also struck up a close relationship with W.A. Gardener, who, like Van Horne, rose to meteoric heights in the railway world. At this time Gardener was a telegraph operator in Bloomington, but by 1912 he was president of the Chicago and Northwestern Railway and the St. Paul, Minneapolis & Omaha Railway. Another friend from Bloomington was Peter Whitman, a lumber dealer who went on to become a large manufacturer and, finally, a bank president. But men on the rise seldom have the opportunity to stay long in one place and, all too soon, Van Horne was on the move again — this time to Alton, Illinois, to take up a new job with the Chicago and Alton.

By the time that he left Bloomington, Van Horne had established a solid foundation for his railway career. He was not only rising in a cutting-edge industry that was strategically situated in both the American economy and the Midwest, but he had attained that most desirable of all Victorian goals — bourgeois respectability. As the son of a middle-class, professional father, and now a married man with a family himself, he was ready to capitalize on his exceptional skills and advance quickly up the railway hierarchy.

3

Realizing a Dream

Van Horne's dream of becoming general superintendent of a railway came closer to being a reality when, on May 1, 1868, he was appointed head of the Chicago and Alton's entire telegraph system, making him one of the railway's two assistant supervisors. In this new role he came into frequent contact with the company's leading officials, who were soon impressed by both his bearing and his force of character. Within a few months they offered him a position with even greater authority: superintendent of the railway's new southern division. Van Horne promptly accepted. And so it was that, in 1869, he moved his entire family to Alton, Illinois. Like the modern-day diplomat's or serviceman's family that finds itself on the move every two or three years, the Van Hornes soon learned that they had to be prepared to pack and move on short notice.

The family was even larger now than in 1867, when it first came together in Bloomington. The following year William and

Addie welcomed their first-born child, Adaline, whom they affectionately called Little Addie. In later years, this devoted daughter would grow to more than six feet in height and would resemble her father in girth. And, like him, she would develop an excellent head for business, a love of art, and a passion for collecting things. But she was only an infant when the family arrived in Alton, a hilly river town that sits on limestone bluffs overlooking the meandering Mississippi River, some twenty miles north of St. Louis, Missouri. When the Van Hornes moved there, the town had stately homes on lovely, wide, tree-shaded streets and was quickly attracting heavy industry, thanks to its excellent railway facilities and Mississippi River location.

Van Horne had already bought a ten-room brick house on a "pretty street" that enjoyed a spectacular view of the city and of the river for miles around. He wrote to Addie that it was a little larger than the family required, but he was sure it would please her. It certainly suited him because he was developing a taste for large residences. In fact, in later life he would confess that he liked his homes "fat and bulgy like [himself]."

Van Horne's new responsibilities at the Chicago and Alton Railroad included the day-to-day movement of all passengers and freight over the southern division, the discipline and conduct of its employees, the hiring of agents, and the maintenance of the division's structures and equipment. These duties presented a daunting challenge for a young man who had just turned twenty-six. He relished his new job, however, because not only did it broaden his railway experience, but it also placed him on the direct line of authority from Timothy Blackstone, a former railway engineer turned astute businessman who was now the company president. As an assistant superintendent, Van Horne reported to the superintendent, who, in turn, reported to Blackstone. Blackstone had been promoted to the presidency only three months after being appointed a director in 1864. At the time, the Chicago and Alton was in poor shape. But he used his managerial expertise to turn the railway's fortunes around and pave the way for the Chicago and Alton to become one of the most profitable of American railways.

Closer to home, in Alton, Van Horne came under the close observation of John Mitchell, a prominent western railroading man and a director of the Chicago and Alton. Given Van Horne's driving ambition and talents, he would have advanced rapidly up the railway hierarchy, but his progress was aided and abetted in no small part by the interest that Blackstone and Mitchell took in his career.

In 1870, impressed by Van Horne's enthusiasm, industry, and administrative skills, the company promoted him to its headquarters in Chicago. There he became an assistant superintendent in charge of the movement of passengers and freight over the entire Chicago and Alton system. In this new position he would strive to beat all the competition by stressing efficiency and streamlining operations as much as possible.

Van Horne was no doubt delighted to be back in Chicago, a lake port with a population of some three hundred thousand people and railway links to both coasts. Situated at the mouth of the Chicago River at the southwest corner of Lake Michigan, it had grown from its humble beginnings in 1830 into a vital transshipment centre for grain, livestock, and lumber from the Midwest. When Van Horne returned to this vibrant, raw-boned city in 1870, it boasted factories, grain elevators, wholesale houses, the sprawling Union Stock Yards, and even a few private libraries and the Chicago Academy of Design. But Chicago, like so many other frontier towns, was also awash in gambling establishments, saloons, and houses of prostitution. And worse, it was crowded with wooden structures. Two-thirds of its buildings were made of wood, many of them cheaply constructed. The city's wooden buildings, wooden sidewalks, wood-paved streets, and wooden bridges all created the ideal conditions for a major fire.

On the evening of October 8, 1871, following an exceptionally dry summer, a fire of unknown origin broke out in the city. It was contained, but the next night another fire erupted about a mile and a half southwest of the city centre. This conflagration was not contained, and it quickly spread to neighbouring buildings. Lashed by a strong southwest wind, it ripped through dry wooden shanties and then crossed the Chicago River to the city's south side. From there, it tore like a tornado through the business district to the northeast, demolishing everything in its path.

When this second fire began around nine o'clock on a Sunday night, Addie Van Horne was recovering from delivering their second child, William (Willie), born twenty-four hours earlier. Van Horne was at home, celebrating the arrival of a son and fretting about his wife's condition, when he learned that the fire was rapidly approaching the Union Depot. Despite concerns about his family's fate, he set off immediately to rescue what Chicago and Alton equipment he could.

After hurrying to the freight depot, located in Chicago's West Division, Van Horne arranged with the few employees still around to clear the company's sheds. Most of the rolling stock had already been removed for safety reasons, but he obtained a Chicago, Milwaukee & St. Paul shunting engine and several flat cars to transport any remaining freight that could be rescued. He then circulated among the crowds of people on the Jackson Street Bridge, offering $5 an hour to any man who would help him to load freight onto the flat cars. Many accepted the offer, but before long they would leave the station to watch the fire's progress. Between attempting to keep his recruits at work and rushing out to waylay more help, Van Horne was almost beside himself, but he eventually succeeded in moving the freight to a safe location five miles away. When he set out to pay the workers who had stayed on the job, he could not find them — they had evaporated, never to return for their money. Satisfied that there was nothing more he could do to protect the Chicago and Alton's property, he finally set off for home.

To reach his house in Chicago's South Division, Van Horne had to make his way through a city that appeared to be an inferno of blazing buildings and sidewalks. Smoke, sparks, and flying pieces of burnt lumber, shingles, and roofing were everywhere. So were fear-crazed humans and beasts. He navigated through throngs of people, their faces blackened and blood stained, all trying to escape with the few precious possessions they had managed to save. The streets were an obstacle course of squealing rats smoked from their holes and desperate horses stampeding through the city, most having broken away from their drivers or escaped from city stables. It was a trip he would never forget.

When he finally arrived home, Van Horne was blackened from head to foot, but safe. Addie and the rest of the family had also been spared. He immediately gathered up some bedding and clothes and, assisted by his mother, loaded them onto a grocer's wagon he commandeered and dispatched it to the shivering refugees camped in a nearby park.

Soon after the Chicago fire, Van Horne accepted an offer from the Chicago and Alton to manage one of its smaller subsidiaries, the struggling St. Louis, Kansas City & Northern Railroad. He became superintendent of the five-hundred-and-eighty-one-mile-long road on July 15, 1872, at an annual salary of $5,000. At the young age of twenty-nine he had realized his dream of becoming a railway superintendent — perhaps the youngest railway superintendent in the world.

For the next two years, St. Louis, Missouri — Chicago's arch-rival in the Midwest — became the family home. A cosmopolitan community and a commercial metropolis, St. Louis had been the leading city in the region before the Civil War. With the advent of hostilities and the cessation of Mississippi River traffic from the South, however, it lost ground to Chicago. By the time the Van Hornes took up residence in the summer of 1872, though, the city boasted a population of more than three hundred thousand and was expanding rapidly in all directions. It was also experiencing a golden age that would last until the turn of the century.

In what had become an established practice, Van Horne went ahead of the family to scout out a new home. He settled on an elegant new house in a "very good neighbourhood," with ten rooms, two storeys, and a mansard roof. It was, he reported, "as good as any in the city."

House hunting, of course, was only a diversion. Most of the time Van Horne was preoccupied with settling into his new job. He wrote to Addie, "I leave early tomorrow morning by special train for a trip over the line with the genl frt. agent, chief engineer & asst. genl supt. Mr. Blackstone will go part way with us & Mr. Mitchell will join us tomorrow somewhere on the line. My advent at the North Mo. office caused something of a sensation among the *fossils*. Everything promises well." Evidently, the young superintendent's innovative methods and no-nonsense approach to doing things were starting to make waves.

Later that summer Van Horne was the central figure in a little drama whose outcome would further embellish his growing reputation. He was on an inspection trip in the Midwest when four seedy-looking young men began slapping a small, petrified black child who had begun wailing in response to their loud, boisterous conversation. The terrified mother pleaded with them to stop, but to no avail. Van Horne, who had been watching the altercation with mounting fury, leapt out of his seat, grabbed one of the assailants by the collar, and pulled him into the aisle. "Leave that child alone," he barked.

"All right, Capt'n," sputtered the ruffian as he made his way back to his seat. By the time the train pulled into the station, however, this unsavoury character had regained his nerve, and he turned on Van Horne belligerently. His companions intervened and dragged him off the train just as the conductor suddenly appeared and warned Van Horne to duck down. "Don't you know who these men are?" he whispered. "That's Jessie and Frank James and the Young brothers. Stay where you are or they may decide to aim a shot or two at you as the train leaves." Although somewhat shaken, Van Horne pretended that he had not just encountered the well-known American outlaw and that nothing out of the ordinary had happened.

Once installed in his new job, Van Horne tried to make the railway's equipment more efficient, to save money and to get the best performance out of his employees. He badgered the owners to purchase steel rails, which were far more durable and had a much higher load capacity than the standard iron ones. He also demanded that his employees adopt money-saving measures whenever possible and perform to the best of their ability. However, although he was a strict disciplinarian and a hard taskmaster, Van Horne was no bully. He never asked an employee to put in as many hours of service as he did himself. Moreover, he sympathized with the plight of those railroading men who had to spend long periods of time away from their families. To make them comfortable when they were on the road, he established clubs and reading rooms at divisional points. But he had no sympathy for a drunken employee. When this kind of misbehaviour occurred, he would "cuss out" the offender with great energy and effectiveness.

On one occasion he dismissed a St. Louis, Kansas City & Northern engineer for being drunk on the job, and immediately the Brotherhood of Engineers went on strike. When Van Horne hired an efficient substitute, the union labelled him a strikebreaker and a scab. Despite the uproar, Van Horne refused to discharge him or to reinstate his predecessor. He informed the union leaders bluntly, "The Chicago and Alton have had their nose brought down to the grindstone too often, and they are not going to do it this time if I can help it."

In the long and bitter struggle that followed, the strikers often indulged in ruthless sabotage. Van Horne, who enjoyed a good fight, refused to back down. For weeks on end he worked inhuman hours, astounding staff by his ability to function with so little sleep. Fortunately, the strike ended in a complete victory for him and the company. Nevertheless, peace brought no slackening of discipline. "A railway," he reminded the men, "was no reform school."

On more than one occasion, Van Horne learned of employee misbehaviour by listening to the tapping of a telegraph machine when he was visiting a small station. He was able to decipher the incoming dots and dashes so accurately and administer punishment so swiftly that he earned a reputation for uncanny powers. Years later, when he stopped by the Canadian Pacific Railway's

New York telegraph office, he demonstrated these celebrated powers by deciphering an incoming communication that was addressed to him. "Here is your message," said the clerk.

"Yes, and here is my answer," Van Horne immediately replied. He had been composing his reply as the message came in.

At this stage in his life, Van Horne looked much as he would for the rest of his life. Although not handsome, he was a striking man with fine features and penetrating blue eyes. His nose was small and chiselled, and his short, immaculately trimmed beard suggested a rock-hard jaw beneath it. His hair had already receded back from his high forehead to the middle of his skull, and he would become completely bald in later years. A contemporary described Van Horne as "rather heavy set." With the passage of time he would become decidedly corpulent, but never would his bulk suggest softness. Van Horne, no matter how old, would always radiate strength and power.

Despite his grave manner, Van Horne still retained an impish sense of humour and a love of pranks. When the family lived in Bloomington, he put his artistic talents to work transforming figures in one of his mother's fashion journals into a collection of freaks. In St. Louis he took liberties with some of the artwork reproduced in copies of *Harper's Magazine* that he intercepted before they reached the women at home. He once altered a series of portrait sketches of American authors by Canadian artist Wyatt Eaton in such a way that they appeared to be pictures of cowboys and Indians. The transformation was so convincing that his mother and mother-in-law were thoroughly deceived, protesting that it was scandalous that the editors had allowed esteemed writers such as Longfellow and Emerson to be ridiculed. Even Eaton was deceived when somebody showed him the distorted illustrations.

When the family was living in St. Louis, Addie came down with smallpox — then one of the most deadly and loathsome of diseases. In the nineteenth century it was customary to isolate smallpox patients in a "pesthouse," but Van Horne would have none of that for his beloved wife. Putting an end to all discussion, he proceeded to care for her himself in the attic study where he kept his fossil collection. As long as the illness lasted, he whiled away his days in this sanctuary, devotedly nursing her and amusing himself with his fossils. When night came and she slept, he changed his clothing, thoroughly disinfected himself, and set off for his deserted office to attend to the day's work. That done, he would return to the study in the early hours of the morning to snatch some sleep himself. It was a punishing regimen, but Van Horne had the satisfaction of seeing his wife make a splendid recovery with few, if any, disfiguring scars. Moreover, because of the precautions he adopted, nobody else in the house contracted this extremely contagious disease.

After two years of his resourceful and energetic management, Van Horne decided to leave the St. Louis, Kansas City & Northern Railroad. On June 28, 1874, he told Addie that he intended to submit his resignation the following day. "The bitter feeling towards the Chicago & Alton & everyone who was ever connected with it is the principal cause," he wrote. "This together with the ill feeling of those interested in this company who are also interested in some of the 'side shows' — branch lines etc and whose toes have been trodden on has made my position since the election very unpleasant." Soon after he penned this letter, the company's board of directors met and unanimously recorded "their high appreciation of his faithful and industrious administration of the duties of his office." They then authorized the president to grant him a month's salary as severance pay.

For the first time in over fifteen years Van Horne was unemployed. The hard-driving, thirty-one-year-old executive found the transition difficult, and he sunk into a bout of self-questioning and despondency. That summer, while his wife and children were visiting Bloomington and Joliet, Van Horne found the family home in St. Louis so desolate and cheerless that he wrote to Addie: "Whatever misfortunes may come in a business way I cannot be unhappy while my dear treasures are left to me. You cannot imagine how lonely I feel without you here. Sometimes I feel as if I could fly to you." The once confident railway official even began to question whether his future lay in railroading.

At that point John Mitchell came to the rescue. As a director of the Chicago and Alton, he had become aware of a small, financially weak railway that a man with Van Horne's expertise might be able to save — the Southern Minnesota Railroad. This unfinished railway ran from the Wisconsin-Minnesota boundary opposite La Crosse, Wisconsin, westward through one hundred and sixty-seven miles of sparsely settled southern Minnesota to Winnebago City. When Mitchell learned that the Southern Minnesota was in receivership, he persuaded its New York bondholders that Van Horne was just the person to build up the line and transform it into a profitable enterprise. He then persuaded Van Horne to leave St. Louis and become general manager of the Southern Minnesota, whose offices were located in La Crosse, a Mississippi River town that owed much of its prosperity to the lumber industry.

When Van Horne took over the management of the railway on October 1, 1874, he faced an intimidating challenge: to increase the company's earnings so it could meet its expenses and interest charges and, at the same time, pay off its old debts and free the railway's right-of-way of the claims against it. He had to meet this challenge at a time of crippling depression in the country, brought on by the 1873 failure of banker Jay Cooke.

With his characteristic gusto, Van Horne set out to turn around the fortunes of the railway. It took him about three years to accomplish this goal — years of frustration, setbacks, and triumph. He recorded the highlights of these years in large letter books which reveal the vital role that correspondence played in the years before the telephone linked major centres. When not on the road, Van Horne often wrote letters every day to his reporting superior, Cornelius Gold, the head of the Southern Minnesota's executive committee and later the railway's president. When major developments were breaking, he often dispatched two letters a day to this New York–based official. And, in addition to this correspondence, Van Horne would fire off missives to other railroading officials and colleagues, always in his own handwriting.

The first change Van Horne made at the Southern Minnesota was to replace some of the key staff with men who had worked with him before. Next he introduced stringent economies and settled all the outstanding claims for the right of way by dealing directly with the owners. By August 1876, less than two years after he became manager, he was able to predict a surplus for the coming three months that would make a "big hole" in the claims against the railway. Looking to the future, Van Horne had new snow fences built along the track and improved the railway's rolling stock and roadbed. The following year he spent lavishly on repairs to the track, bridges, and roadbed and in the construction of new buildings. And he accomplished all these improvements despite periodic rate wars that were designed to grab business from competing divisions of rival railways.

Wheat was the principal commodity carried by the railway, so Van Horne offered inducements for the erection of flour mills and suitable grain elevators along the line. In order to restrain competition and to further increase the Southern Minnesota's earnings, he arranged with rival lines to divide either the traffic or the earnings realized from the traffic of the participating railways.

In the summer of 1876, however, the Southern Minnesota faced a natural calamity of nature's making — a plague of Rocky Mountain locusts (commonly known as grasshoppers) that wreaked havoc in northern Minnesota before moving into the southern part of the state. As the insects moved from east to west, they dropped periodically to the surrounding fields to lay their eggs and munch their way through huge swaths of wheat and other grains. Van Horne knew that depleted wheat crops spelled smaller freight loads for the railway, and that deposited eggs would invariably hatch the following spring to unleash new destruction. While farm families offered up public prayers for the banishment of this "terrible engine of destruction," Van Horne used his ingenuity to devise an effective "hopperdozer" to destroy the pests. This invention — a piece of sheet iron or stretched canvas thickly smeared with tar — was dragged through an infected field by a horse. When the disturbed grasshoppers flew upwards from the ground, they become entangled in the tar. Farmers eagerly adopted Van Horne's invention, the state supplied free tar, and the Southern Minnesota cooperated by carrying both the iron and the tar free of charge. Soon Van Horne had the satisfaction of seeing huge heaps of dead hoppers dotting the prairie.

The general manager knew that good staff morale was essential to efficiency and productivity, and he did everything he could to foster it. He believed that tasty, well-prepared food was a powerful inducement to performance on the job, and he made it clear that no eating house along the line would be patronized unless it provided the best possible meals. Frequently he carried out taste tests himself when he was on the road, telegraphing an order to the next eating stop for two dinners — and then devouring them both. If his appetite was prodigious, so was his energy. A glutton for work, Van Horne toiled away in his office from nine-thirty or ten in the morning until eleven or twelve at night, taking time off only for dinner.

As part of a program to involve every employee in the Southern Minnesota's regeneration, he introduced contests in many areas of the railway's operations, from track repairing to engine driving. He gave a prize, along with a personal letter from him, to every man who did the best work at the least cost. The Southern Minnesota's auditor recalled that "Van Horne created on that old Minnesota Road an esprit de corps rarely equalled.... We had to look twice at every cent. But we all enjoyed working on that road. Van Horne was full of ways to get around difficulties, and as full of ideas for improving every branch of the work."

After three full years with the Southern Minnesota, Van Horne was shocked when Peter Myers, his highly respected vice-president, threatened to resign because of inadequate pay. Van Horne immediately resolved to make more money available for salary increases by taking a cut in his own pay. As he wrote to Myers, "I have thought it all over and made up my mind to reduce my own salary materially on January 1st [1878] no matter what action the board takes in regard to the others."

Van Horne's efforts to rehabilitate the line soon began to pay off. Gross earnings for the first year of his management were the highest in the railway's history. Moreover, operating expenses had slid from 72 to 56 percent of earnings, and there was a respectable sum in the railway's coffers.

Van Horne also mounted a tireless campaign to have the Southern Minnesota extend its line westward, believing that strategic expansion was essential if his railway was to keep ahead of its competitors. The executive committee's failure to act swiftly on the matter was a source of great frustration to him, especially after he realized that a "good class" of settlers were pouring into the country west of the Southern Minnesota and that, if his company did not push a line through to this part of the state, another railway would. Still, he was not prepared to see an extension built on just any terms. If it could not be constructed with lightly bonded debt and aid voted by the towns it would serve, he preferred not to build it at all. His strenuous lobbying finally persuaded the powers-that-be to extend the line westward by means of a separate company organized for this purpose. Van Horne was appointed vice-president of the Southern Minnesota Extension Company, and his friend and occasional business associate, Jason Easton, president.

Construction of the new line began in February 1878, after extensive surveys had been carried out. Van Horne scrutinized every aspect of the work closely, even the locating and naming of stations. Whenever a Native association still persisted, he incorporated it in that name. One such place was Pipestone, where Native Americans, observing an ancient custom, still assembled once a year to collect red stone for making peace pipes.

The building of the extension involved Van Horne in much more than construction matters. He also had to organize a company to build it, chase funds, and lobby for a charter and for the transfer of the railway's lapsed land grant to the new company. It would have been much easier to hire a lawyer or a legislator to act as a lobbyist for the company, but, to save money, Van Horne took on all these tasks himself. Immersing himself in railway law and sharpening his powers of persuasion, he plunged into what had previously been a completely foreign world to him — state politics. When legislation of interest to the Southern Minnesota Railroad was debated in the Minnesota legislature, he made frequent trips to the state capital, St. Paul. There, in the state legislature's smoke-filled committee rooms and crowded corridors, he sought out key politicians and attempted to enlighten them about the Minnesota's needs and aspirations. The first round of lobbying took place in 1876 and involved an extension of the company's lapsed land grant. He got what he wanted. Another round of strenuous politicking began in the early months of 1878. This time Van Horne lobbied vigorously to have the Minnesota legislature turn over the railway's land grant to the newly formed extension company. The ensuing struggle, waged against a background of competing railway interests, soon developed into open warfare. Eventually, however, after much arm-twisting by Van Horne, the Minnesota bill was passed.

During these visits to the Minnesota state capital, Van Horne was forced to hobnob with a variety of lobbyists and other prominent railwaymen of the West. Some of them later described him as a "man of commanding intellect and energy, who knew what he knew for certain," but who could combine persuasion with diplomacy and tact. However, despite his many political successes, Van Horne was not enamoured of the game of politics. To the end of his life he disliked both politics and the men who practised it.

Attracting settlers was another challenge Van Horne faced. He was shrewd enough to realize that settlers cultivating the soil and creating traffic for the railway were far more important to the long-term interests of the company than the dollars earned from land sales. Consequently, he assigned top priority to attracting good settlers, or, as he phrased it, the "good class of people" then being settled on the Minnesota prairie by the noted prelate John Ireland, coadjutor bishop of St. Paul. Van Horne had been greatly impressed by the idealistic bishop — the founder of a colonization bureau that was busily establishing rural villages and farming communities.

When hordes of settlers and land-hunters began to arrive in the southwestern part of Minnesota, Van Horne fought hard to have his railway reduce the steep prices it was charging for its lands. "It is humiliating, to say the least," he wrote to Cornelius Gold, "to see hundreds of settlers going west every day and be unable to stop one in a thousand of them." To attract settlers he devised a scheme in which they received credits for breaking and seeding their land within a specified period of time. Credits acquired in this way could be applied to the first payment due on a piece of land. The scheme proved to be such a powerful sales tool that land sales along the extension multiplied rapidly. Before long, all these new settlements were generating traffic for the Southern Minnesota.

By the spring and summer of 1878, Van Horne was preoccupied with plans for his future. Recognized as one of the ablest railway operators in the country — in the words of one railroading man as "bigger than his job" — it is not surprising that other railways were competing for his talents. In early 1878, for example, the Chicago and Alton Railroad tried to lure him away from the Southern Minnesota, and the latter strove valiantly to keep him. As he tried to evaluate the merits of the rival proposals, Van Horne was plunged into agonies of indecision and fretting.

As usual, when weighing questions of importance he turned for comfort and advice to Addie. In March he told her that it would be in his best interest to accept the Chicago and Alton offer, yet his present employer had proposed that he become both general manager and president and accept a boost in salary. Addie sympathized with his predicament, but, ultimately, she said, Van Horne alone could make the decision. He resolved his quandary by agreeing to stay on as general manager with the Southern Minnesota and to take on the additional office of president later in the year.

There was also the question of Addie's health. She had been failing for a year or more, no doubt because of the loss of their beloved son, Willie, who died at five years of age (the cause of death is not known). The sudden death of this "bright and lovely little sunbeam" on May 17, 1876, was a terrible blow for both parents, even after the arrival of a second son, Richard Benedict

Bennie Van Horne, Van Horne's only surviving son. Although very gifted, he failed to realize his potential and to live up to his father's demanding expectations.

Courtesy of Library and Archives Canada, E000945218.

(Bennie), the following May. Van Horne was convinced that his wife's deteriorating health would improve only if the family moved to a better climate. And so, when he received an invitation to become general manager of the Chicago and Alton, he accepted the offer. The family, except for his sister Mary, who remained at teachers' college in La Crosse, prepared to move to Chicago. Van Horne did not sever his connection with the Minnesota railway entirely, however, as he kept on as president and as a director. This arrangement allowed him to continue directing the progress of the extension, which eventually terminated in Flandreau, North Dakota.

Van Horne's years with the Southern Minnesota Railroad gave him the varied experience and the connections he needed to advance his career to the highest levels. Through Peter Myers and Jason Easton he had learned a great deal about railway financing, and in building the extension he had broadened his knowledge not only of construction but also of lobbying and politics. At the same time he had rescued an obscure railway from bankruptcy and transformed it into a paying property. As a result of this major achievement, and his earlier turnaround of the St. Louis, Kansas City & Northern Railroad, he now enjoyed an excellent reputation among his railroading colleagues. It was a reputation to be proud of — and one that stood him in good stead when he took on the new challenges that awaited him.

4

New Challenges and Hobbies

Van Horne was thirty-five years old when he was lured back to the Chicago and Alton in October 1878. When he first joined the railway over fifteen years earlier, it had been as a telegraph operator and a ticket agent. With this most recent appointment, he became the general superintendent of an important, well-established railway.

Given his reputation for innovation in railway operations, news of his appointment struck fear in the hearts of many men at the Chicago and Alton. Once he had taken up his new post, however, conscientious employees found that they had no reason to be alarmed. As one railroading man later summed up the situation, "Everybody thought Van Horne would tear things. Everybody looked for lightning to strike. Even the general manager was disturbed over his appointment. But Van Horne went his gait in a characteristic go-ahead style, invariably hitting it right."

The railway that Van Horne rejoined was a prosperous, efficient company that hauled more coal into Chicago than any other railway. It was also a prime mover of corn, wheat, and livestock from its Kansas City terminal. But to achieve and maintain this position it waged a ceaseless war with other railways for traffic, particularly after the depression of the mid-1870s resulted in decreased freight. With his combative temperament, high energy, and willingness to experiment with new methods, Van Horne was ideally suited to this type of competition. He plunged joyously into the struggle, waging such a successful battle for business that he attracted the attention of the heads of other more important railways.

To attract passengers, Van Horne naturally thought of food — as he had done earlier in his career to keep workers happy. Departing from common practice, he arranged for the railway to own and operate its own dining cars, rather than use those supplied by the celebrated Pullman Car Company. Once the cars arrived, he instructed the Chicago and Alton staff to serve more generous portions than the Pullman people did. Car construction was another interest of Van Horne's. On his frequent visits to the company's car shops, Van Horne often passed on new ideas to the designers and builders. If they could not readily grasp what he had in mind, he illustrated his concepts with sketches. When new mail cars were required, he dispatched the Chicago and Alton's master car builder to Washington to learn from the general superintendent of the United States mail service how best to equip a mail car. In this area, as in all departments, he revealed an obsession with detail and quality. He was lavish in his praise of good work, but he could also be scathing in his denunciation of inferior results and performance. Confronted by a poor performance, he would go to considerable lengths to see that his staff measured up to his expectations.

Although the young dynamo appeared virtually invincible to his fellow railroaders, he was not always successful. On one high-profile occasion involving the travel plans of Rutherford B. Hayes, the U.S. president, he was soundly beaten by a rival railway. After winding up a tour of the West in 1878, Hayes decided that he would travel from Kansas City to his hometown — Fremont, Ohio — via Illinois. His staff asked the Chicago and Alton to furnish a special train for the journey, and the company was only too happy to oblige. It entrusted the arrangements to Van Horne, who quickly assembled the finest cars he could lay his hands on and engaged a renowned Chicago restaurant to provide the meals. To all appearances everything was in order when Van Horne and his New York stockbroker friend George B. Hopkins left Chicago for Kansas City, where the president and his party were to board the train. At about five o'clock the following morning, as this train stood in the Kansas City terminal yards, Van Horne rose, dressed, and went outside for a stroll. Passing the telegraph office, he heard telegraph keys tapping out his name. Intrigued, he stopped to listen. The deciphered message revealed that a rival railway official had surreptitiously arranged for one of his own trains to take the president's party across Illinois. The elated sender, delirious with joy at his success, closed his message with the words, "Van Horne will be as mad as hell."

Van Horne was indeed furious. Nevertheless, there was nothing he could do except watch President Hayes arrive at Kansas City and leave for Fremont on the rival railway's train. Stung to the quick and mortified beyond belief, he returned to the Chicago and Alton's train. But he did not lose his cool in front of his friend. In a remarkable demonstration of self-control, he merely mentioned the rival railway's coup as they as made their lonely way back from Kansas City to Chicago. But then he spotted his chance to get his own back. Crowds of people had assembled at small western stations to cheer the president on his way. So he persuaded Hopkins, who had worn a formal frock coat for this splendid occasion, to pretend that he was President Hayes and to wave to the eager onlookers — We must not disappoint the loyal citizens, Van Horne argued. As the handsome, suitably attired Hopkins stood on the train's rear platform and graciously greeted the waiting throngs of people, they were just as impressed by him as they would have been by the president himself. Between these appearances, Van Horne and his friend enjoyed the abundance of fine food at their disposal. They sat down to a sumptuous dinner, with twenty-five waiters in attendance and a chef and five assistants to supply their every whim!

The climax came when the Chicago and Alton special train met up with its rival at an Illinois junction. There, Van Horne encountered General William Tecumseh Sherman, the commanding general of the U.S. Army. Sherman, who was travelling with the president's entourage, entered Van Horne's car to beg for a Scotch and soda, complaining that he had been travelling with the teetotalling president for four days without so much as one drink. Once satisfied, he invited Van Horne to go with him to meet Hayes, but the still aggrieved Van Horne declined. Finally, Sherman made his way back to his train, only to return with the president, who said how much he regretted the mix-up. News of the incident circulated widely in railroading circles, where rival railroaders crowed over the humbling of the hitherto invincible Van Horne. Before long, however, Van Horne regarded it all as a great joke — and dined out on the story countless times.

Although his new position at the Chicago and Alton was demanding, Van Horne still found time to add more specimens to his fossil collection. His passion for fossils had become widely known, and all along the railway lines the men kept an eye out for finds that might interest him. He also devoted leisure hours to another favourite pursuit — gardening. He had taken up this hobby at La Crosse, determined to produce larger and more luxurious flowers than his neighbours. In his quest for the perfect bloom, Van Horne dug his own beds, studied fertilizers, carefully tended each and every plant himself, and walked long distances on the Bluffs to obtain leaf mould for his roses. In Chicago he cultivated tulips and hyacinths in the attic and cellars of the family's large brick home at 48 Park Avenue.

This spacious, rambling house may have been to Van Horne's liking, but it did not please Addie. She was dismayed by the profusion of halls and predicted that their new home would be difficult to keep clean. "I wish I were back in our house [in La Crosse] a thousand times," she wrote plaintively to her sister-in-law Mary in October 1878. This second Chicago interlude would be a trying one for Addie in other ways as well. She was still mourning her son Willie and enduring the long bout of ill health that followed his death. Chicago's changeable climate, with its abundance of cool, windy weather, was another irritant, as were her husband's many absences from home.

Most of Van Horne's time away from Chicago was taken up with visits to La Crosse, where, in his continuing role as president of the Southern Minnesota, he oversaw the completion of the railway's extension. He also had private business to conduct because he had invested in a few properties there, including a farm. Although he was still in his thirties, he was already taking the first steps towards becoming a financier.

Van Horne had been managing the Chicago and Alton for only one year when he accepted an offer to be general superintendent of still another railway — the Chicago, Milwaukee & St. Paul Railroad, a rapidly expanding company with extensive mileage in Wisconsin, Illinois, Iowa, the Dakotas, Minnesota, and Missouri. His remarkable success in resurrecting the Southern Minnesota and the tenacity and resourcefulness with which he had waged the Chicago and Alton's ferocious battles for traffic had caught the attention of the Milwaukee management. Van Horne's particular type of genius, they were convinced, was just what was needed to consolidate the numerous railways that the Chicago, Milwaukee & St. Paul was acquiring and to blend them into a harmonious, effective system. Accordingly, the railway offered him the title of general superintendent, but intended to give him all the duties and powers of a general manager. His new appointment was to begin on January 1, 1880.

Van Horne accepted the plum appointment because of the big salary he was offered — it was "a question of dollars and future," he explained. He still felt a sense of loyalty to the Southern Minnesota Railroad and would have turned down the offer had he believed the company was in danger. But he knew that it was now under capable management and in respectable shape. And as the Chicago and Alton Railroad was flourishing, he had no qualms about leaving it.

New Year's Day dawned with the family still in Chicago and Van Horne in Milwaukee, Wisconsin. He had not visited the city before — a beer-brewing capital noted for its bustling port, extensive gardens, and broad streets. He had been warned to expect a frigid reception from the men at the Chicago, Milwaukee & St.

Paul, but he wrote with relief to Addie, "I have been very cordially received here — more cordially than I could have expected in view of the harsh colours in which I have been pictured to the employees. From what I have heard some of them looked for a regular ogre with fangs and fiery breath." Still, it was not all smooth sailing. Although his job qualifications were excellent, several important officials objected strenuously to a new man being placed over them and did not hesitate to express their antagonism. They even encouraged insubordination on the part of younger men. By 1881, though, Van Horne's expertise, inexhaustible patience, natural buoyancy of spirit, and irresistible personality had won over all the disaffected.

During his first year with the Milwaukee railway, it acquired still more small lines. The task of integrating the railway's different branches, such as the Chicago and Pacific, and welding them into one well-coordinated system presented a major challenge. But the most daunting task of all was to reduce the company's operating costs. Here Van Horne started a revolution in the operation of railways, according to an unidentified railroader, and he implemented methods that are still in use today. He taught the railway world how to load freight cars to their fullest capacity and made eight hundred cars do the work previously done by a thousand. He applied similar strictures to engines and all the other equipment. His colleague, Frank Underwood, a future president of the Erie Railroad, reported: "Most of the present, up-to-date methods of transportation were thought out by him. Some of them have been enlarged and improved. The original suggestions, however, were his."

As part of his campaign to streamline operations and reduce costs, Van Horne instituted a comprehensive store and accounting system. First, though, he appointed a three-member committee to study and report on the systems used by other large railways. One of the committee's members was a young clerk, Thomas George Shaughnessy, who would soon play a leading role beside Van Horne in the construction of the Canadian Pacific Railway.

Among Van Horne's many responsibilities was the erection of new stations and buildings. He welcomed this challenge because it involved him in architecture and art — two of his personal passions. Previously, railways had been content to erect cost-saving, efficient buildings. Van Horne, however, aimed to design structures that not only met the requirements of function and economy but also harmonized with their surroundings and appealed to the eye. A typical Van Horne station was a rather Spartan, two-storey building that provided living quarters for the stationmaster and his family on the second floor. Adjoining this utilitarian structure was a one-storey wing where freight could be stored. When the Canadian Pacific Railway was built, many of the depots erected in western Canada would incorporate this basic design.

During his stint at the Chicago, Milwaukee & St. Paul Railroad, the company tried to get possession of a small, obscure line, the Chicago, Rockford & Northern, which was in receivership. The Milwaukee had been in a continuing dispute with this railway's receiver and, to bring the matter to a conclusion, Van Horne resorted to rough-and-tumble tactics. He summoned A.J. Earling, a divisional superintendent, to his office, presented him with a large bundle of documents and correspondence, and ordered him to take possession of the Chicago, Rockford & Northern. He allotted him two engines and twenty men to accomplish the task. After reaching the crossing of the two railways, Earling moved the engines onto the smaller company's line — and there they sat. The receiver attempted to oust the trespassers and recover possession of the line, but he was confronted by Earling, his phalanx of men, and his mountain of documents. The receiver hastened back to Chicago for reinforcements — but Van Horne heard what he was up to and countered with additional men of his own. Both sides proceeded to raise the stakes, until Earling eventually had eight hundred men supporting him on the spot. Five or six times a day he consulted with his boss by telegraph, and Van Horne always responded: "Be sure to have plenty of good provisions for your men. As long as you keep their bellies full, they will remain loyal." Fortified by good food, the Milwaukee squad emerged from a week of enforced idleness and threats with flying colours. Van Horne's road remained in possession of the Chicago, Rockford & Northern. Ultimately, however, the courts decided that the two claimants should have joint use of the disputed line.

Van Horne had been with the Chicago, Milwaukee & St. Paul for just over a year and a half when he was invited to move north to become general manager of the Canadian Pacific Railway. Although he was only thirty-eight, he was already a seasoned railroader whose tenacity, resourcefulness, and capacity for hard work had attracted the attention of senior railroading men in the United States. One of these men, a transplanted Canadian named James Jerome Hill, persuaded the CPR's president, George Stephen, to make the offer that would launch a new chapter in Van Horne's life.

5

Van Horne Moves to Canada

William Van Horne first met James Jerome Hill, an almost mythical American railway magnate, in 1876, when he was busy transforming the small, bankrupt Southern Minnesota Railroad into a paying property. Hill, who had settled in St. Paul, Minnesota, was then reorganizing the St. Paul, Minneapolis & Manitoba Railway with the aid of several associates, two of whom — Donald Smith and George Stephen — were Scottish Canadians. Hill quickly became Van Horne's mentor and friend. That they were attracted to each other is not surprising. Both were driven, gifted, practical railroading men with inquiring minds, amazing stamina, a strong aesthetic streak, and a passion for art. They even bore a striking physical resemblance to each other — stocky, bald, and barrel-chested.

In 1881 it was Hill who suggested to George Stephen, the CPR's president, that Van Horne be invited to become general

Courtesy of Library and Archives Canada, C6654.

James J. Hill, empire builder of the American Northwest and Van Horne's friend and arch railroading rival.

manager of the fledgling company, incorporated earlier that same year. Relatively little of the CPR's main line had been built by then, and the CPR syndicate was eager to see the pace of construction speeded up. "You need a man of great mental and physical power to carry this line through," Hill wrote to Stephen. "Van Horne can do it. But he will take all the authority he gets and more, so define how much you want him to have." Van Horne was indeed the ideal choice for pushing through the construction of the railway. For one thing, he had a practical knowledge of almost every department of railway work, from the construction of bridges or the laying of curves to the management of an extensive system. He also had the ability to make tough decisions, an asset that would prove indispensable to building the CPR.

The construction of a transcontinental railway had been a central issue in Canada ever since Confederation in 1867. Many people all across the wide, sparsely populated country believed that a ribbon of steel was essential to the survival of the fragile Canadian union. The framers of the British North America Act had even incorporated the Intercolonial Railway in Canada's constitution, and the terms of British Columbia's entry into Confederation in 1871 also contained a provision calling for the construction of a transcontinental line.

The new federal government had been able to complete the eastern section of the project quite easily by finishing the construction of the Intercolonial Railway in 1876, the first through-train arriving at Quebec from Halifax on July 6 of that year. The western section would pose far more problems and take much longer to complete. Prime Minister Sir John A. Macdonald made the first attempt, placing a privately owned syndicate headed by the wealthy shipping magnate Sir Hugh Allan in charge. The entire enterprise soon collapsed, however, when it was reported that Allan had contributed large sums of money to Macdonald's party during the hard-fought election campaign of 1872. The eruption of the "Pacific Scandal" and the findings of a royal commission that implicated Macdonald and his Quebec lieutenant, Sir George-Étienne Cartier, forced Macdonald to resign in late 1873.

Surveys of potential routes and piecemeal construction continued, however, under the Liberal government of Alexander Mackenzie (1873–78). Although his administration adopted a more cautious fiscal policy, it nevertheless spent 25 percent of its budget on surveys and construction in one year alone, 1875.

By the time that Macdonald and the Conservatives returned to power in 1878, British Columbia was threatening to secede from Confederation if all the terms of its admission to Canada were not met. As if to underscore the seriousness of its threat, it sent a provincial delegation to London in the spring of 1881 to seek a repeal of the union. Macdonald wasted no time in swinging into action, realizing full well that the province might leave the union. Even if it did not, an American railway near the international border could siphon off western Canada's commerce by constructing spur lines northward. Hill's St. Paul, Minneapolis & Manitoba Railway, which linked St. Paul with St. Vincent, Minnesota, at the Manitoba border, was a case in point. The possible invasion of the southern prairies by an American railway was not the only factor that had to be considered. There was also Canadians' pride, their nationalism, their determination not to become Americans. Macdonald knew that any future transcontinental line between Montreal and the Pacific had to be an all-Canadian railway and not simply a connection with a line bending north from the mid-western United States.

To construct the transcontinental, Macdonald and the Conservatives decided to have a private company build and operate the railway, but with some government assistance. Their choice was the one group that appeared to have the necessary resources and credentials to carry out such an intimidating undertaking — James Hill and his St. Paul associates. Eager to snare the CPR contract, they had formed a syndicate in October 1880 for that very purpose.

Heading the consortium was George Stephen, who resigned as president of the Bank of Montreal to lead the new company. This self-confident financier and shrewd negotiator would handle the CPR's budget and governmental relations, assisted by Richard (R.B.) Angus, general manager of the Bank of Montreal. Another prominent syndicate member was Stephen's cousin, Donald Smith, a newly defeated Conservative member of parliament and a senior Hudson's Bay Company official. The company also included James Hill, who would focus on construction and operations; the ineffectual vice-president Duncan McIntyre, who controlled the Canada Central Railway; and a number of bankers from New York and Europe.

Although Macdonald detested Donald Smith and knew that westerners reviled the monopoly held by the Canadian Pacific Railway, he pressed ahead with the "Pacific Bill," believing that only this syndicate could get the job done. The legislation that passed in the House of Commons on January 27, 1881, required the Canadian Pacific Railway to build a railway within ten years and to operate it "in perpetuity" from Callander, Ontario, to Port Moody on Vancouver Island. In return, the Canadian government would grant the company $25 million, twenty-five million acres of land, the lines already under construction (including the Pembina line and railway sections in the Fraser Canyon built by the American contractor Andrew Onderdonk), a twenty-five-year monopoly over running rights in western Canada to the United States, and generous tax and customs concessions.

Van Horne could be impetuous at times, but, before accepting the syndicate's offer, he first made a reconnaissance trip north of the border in October 1881. Evidently he was impressed by what he saw, particularly by the quality of the grain on the gently rolling prairie and the abundance of the crops grown by the Red River settlers in their lush, green fields. All this augured well, he thought, for the future of traffic carried by a transcontinental train. On his return home, he wrote to Hill and accepted the CPR's offer. He knew that his prospects for advancement in the United States were excellent — that he probably could have had the pick of any choice railway position when it became vacant. He also realized, however, that in joining the CPR he was taking on an enormous risk.

The CPR had launched itself on a giant gamble. Its main line was to follow a southern route that required it to penetrate the Rockies and the Selkirk Mountains, located in southeastern British Columbia just west of the Rockies. As yet, however, nobody knew how this feat could be done or even if the track could be pushed through the Selkirks. In addition to these formidable obstacles, there were rivers to be crossed and, in the east, marshy muskegs to be conquered. And, of course, there was the enormous distance that had to be traversed. But Van Horne also knew that an extremely attractive offer was being dangled before him: an annual salary of $15,000, a princely sum for those days. In fact, it would be the largest salary ever paid up to that point to a railway general manager in North America. Still, in accepting the offer Van Horne was probably swayed more by the prospect of a major challenge and his love of adventure than by financial considerations.

Shortly after accepting the CPR's offer, Van Horne moved from Milwaukee to Winnipeg, which would be his home until he relocated to Montreal nine months later. He left his family behind in Milwaukee, where they remained until April 1883, when they joined him in Montreal. This separation was difficult for them all, though he did find time for a few visits home.

Van Horne arrived in Manitoba's raw, infant capital on the last day of 1881, when temperatures were skidding to about forty degrees below zero Fahrenheit and the city was awash in New Year's celebrations. He immediately established his headquarters in a dingy office above the Bank of Montreal, and the next morning he began work. Winnipeg was teeming with new immigrants, many of whom were forced to seek accommodation in the city's immigrant sheds because they could not afford the skyrocketing rates charged by crammed hotels. This overcrowding would make a forceful impression on Van Horne during the time he lived there.

The CPR's decision in 1881 to build its main line through Winnipeg virtually guaranteed that the city would expand at a giddy pace. Waves of farmers and agricultural labourers from Ontario, the United States, and Europe began pouring into Canada's gateway to the West and the adjoining town of St. Boniface. The resulting frenzied land boom was well under way when Van Horne arrived on the scene. That January city lots were flipped like pancakes, selling for double the previous day's price. Before the boom collapsed in late 1882, it would plunge the city into the wildest sixteenth months in its history and help to ignite frantic land speculation in other projected railway towns in Manitoba and the Northwest Territories as well as in Port Moody, British Columbia.

Van Horne was particularly concerned about speculation on land expected to be designated as town sites and CPR stations. Under no circumstances would he tolerate the idea of anybody making a fortune at the CPR's expense. On his first day in his office he placed a small ad in the January 2 Winnipeg

Courtesy of Library and Archives Canada, C33881.

Winnipeg, the gateway to the Canadian West, at about the time Van Horne arrived to take up his job as general manager of the CPR.

newspapers cautioning the public against buying lots expected to be snapped up for stations along the CPR line until he had officially announced their locations. Among those caught up in the orgy of speculation were senior CPR officials based in Winnipeg. Leading the pack was a courtly Southern aristocrat, Thomas Rosser, the CPR's chief engineer. Within a month of assuming his new position, Van Horne not only sacked Rosser but also instructed the superintendent of construction to investigate the source of any continuing leaks of plans and, if necessary, to take the appropriate action.

Van Horne received a frigid reception from his colleagues in Winnipeg. His reputation as a manager who pioneered new ways of doing things in railway operations made tradition-loving railway men resent him. There was also his nationality and his personality: he was a plump, blunt-speaking Yankee who initially hired other Americans whose work he knew and respected. "We did not like Van Horne when he first came up to Winnipeg as General Boss of Everybody & Everything," the locating engineer, an Englishman named J.H. Secretan, wrote in his diary. "His ways were not our ways and he did not hesitate to let us know what he thought of the bunch in a general way." He continued: "At first he had no use for Englishmen or Canadians especially Engineers and told me once 'if he could only teach a Section Man to run a transit he wouldn't have a single d–d Engineer about the place.'"

Van Horne's most important American recruit was Thomas George Shaughnessy, who became the purchasing agent for the entire CPR system in 1882. The job, second only in importance to Van Horne's, would showcase two of Shaughnessy's talents: a remarkable ability to get the best value for every dollar spent, and an equally useful talent for staving off creditors during the railway's construction phase. Hiring Shaughnessy and basing him in Montreal would prove to be one of Van Horne's first strokes of genius after he joined the CPR.

Within ten days of arriving in Winnipeg, Van Horne, accompanied by James Hill and Major A.B. Rogers, the engineer in charge of the CPR's mountain division, journeyed east to Montreal to meet the other syndicate members, and then on to Ottawa to talk to the leading politicians in the nation's capital. At Chicago, where his train stopped while en route to Montreal, Van Horne boldly announced to a newspaper reporter that the CPR intended to construct six hundred and fifty miles of track in 1882. Whether six hundred and fifty or five hundred, the number usually cited in this connection, Van Horne appeared to be promising the impossible.

At the meeting in Montreal, the CPR directors confirmed their choice of a southern route for the railway. This decision meant that the main line would go through Kicking Horse Pass in the Rocky Mountains rather than through the more northerly Yellowhead Pass, which was the choice favoured by Sandford Fleming and other engineers because of its easier grades. In the interests of economy and speed of construction, Van Horne supported the selection of the more steeply graded Kicking Horse Pass and the southern route. He also pitted himself at this meeting against his friend James Hill by arguing forcefully for the immediate construction of the Lake Superior section of the CPR's main line. For his part, Hill vehemently opposed the idea. As he saw it, the forging of an all-Canadian route across the rugged, lake-strewn Shield country north of the Great Lakes was highly impractical. In his opinion, such a line, "when completed would be of no use to anybody and would be a source of heavy loss to whoever operated it." Hill thought that the CPR should build from Callander, Ontario, to Sault Sainte Marie, and from there across a bridge to the U.S. town of Superior-Duluth, and then on to Winnipeg via his own railway, the St. Paul, Minneapolis & Manitoba Railway.

Van Horne found such an idea abhorrent. The last thing he wanted to see was the CPR become dependent on one of Hill's railways, even for a short distance. The transfer of people and freight from one train to another at two points on the journey would be cumbersome, but, most important of all, he was convinced that the difficult lake stretch could not only be built but could be operated profitably. Moreover, he was keenly aware that leading politicians of the day such as Sir John A. Macdonald wanted to see the CPR adopt an all-Canadian route. Hill was furious, and he swore to get even with Van Horne, even if he had "to go to Hell for it and shovel coal." Later, when the decision to build north of Lake Superior was confirmed, Hill formally withdrew from the syndicate. Henceforth he and Van Horne would become bitter railroading rivals. Meanwhile, Van Horne would develop a close friendship with George Stephen, the tall, sartorially elegant president of the CPR.

When Van Horne began his new job early in 1882, the end of track — the site where track was being laid — was at Oak Lake, Manitoba, one hundred and sixty-one miles west of Winnipeg. He intended to build five hundred miles of track that construction season, but that spring it looked as though his plans and his credibility might be torpedoed by dreadful weather conditions. March blizzards were followed by rapidly rising temperatures that quickly thawed the Red River and its tributaries, causing disastrous flood conditions in all their valleys. Large stretches of track were under water, stopping rail traffic for miles around. The resulting massive blockade of traffic choked off the delivery of rail supplies and interfered with the transportation of incoming settlers and their goods. So numerous were the delays that few people believed the CPR could reach its construction goal that season.

The delivery of rail supplies was of particular concern. Before construction of the prairie section began in the late spring, Van Horne had to arrange for the freighting of huge stores of rails and other materials to Winnipeg, the main supply point. The dimensions of this operation were immense. Since the St. Lawrence River would still be frozen when construction began, steel had to be shipped from New York and New Orleans and then hauled to Manitoba via St. Paul. Stone had to be ordered from every available quarry, lumber from Minnesota, railway ties from Lake of the Woods and Rat Portage (now Kenora), and rails from England and the Krupp works in Germany. As general manager, Van Horne had the responsibility for monitoring the whereabouts of these supplies as they made their way from their place of origin to the staging area. He accomplished this overview by arranging for hundreds of checkers to report daily on the arrival and movement of CPR supplies through American cities en route to Winnipeg.

Despite the delay in beginning construction, 1882 saw the completion of four hundred and seventeen miles of main track and twenty-eight more miles of sidings — a truly amazing achievement. By the end of August 1883, the railway stretched all the way from Winnipeg to Keith, ten miles west of Calgary and within sight of the forbidding Rocky Mountains.

To lay the track on the Prairies, a huge construction assembly line extended for a hundred miles or more across the open plains. At its head were CPR engineers and surveyors who located and staked the route that the railway would take. They were followed by grading crews and then the track gangs. To construct the line, the syndicate had hired a company headed by two Minnesota contractors, R.B. Langdon and David Shepard, who in turn parcelled out the work to more than sixty subcontractors.

Determined to speed up operations, Van Horne ordered the track to be advanced at five times the speed that crews had been laying it. During this period of frenzied prairie construction, the general manager seemed to be everywhere. When not doing paperwork in his Winnipeg office, he was out on the Prairies, riding on hand cars or flat cars, in a caboose, or, where the rails had not been laid, in a wagon or a buckboard. Despite his portliness, he moved about continually, "going like a whirlwind wherever he went, stimulating every man he met," reported Angus Sinclair, one of the contractors. Van Horne had a habit of arriving at work sites unexpectedly and descending on local officials like "a blizzard," observed an admiring *Winnipeg Sun* reporter. "He is the terror of Flat Krick. He shakes them up like an earthquake and they are as frightened of him as if he were old Nick himself." Those who saw him in action were constantly amazed by his stamina, to say nothing of his daring. Watching their boss ignore his weight and march across trestles and ties at dizzying heights left all spectators thunderstruck.

To accomplish his goal, Van Horne would summarily dismiss men who were indifferent to their work or not inclined to obey orders. Collingwood Schreiber, the engineer-in-chief for the federal government, recalled that Van Horne would often say to him, "If you want anything done, name the day when it must be finished. If I order a thing done in a specified time and the man to whom I give the order says it is impossible to carry out, *then he must go*. Otherwise his subordinates would make no effort to accomplish the work in the time mentioned." It was a philosophy that served the general manager well.

Van Horne's somewhat autocratic manner and contempt for "the impossible" is well illustrated by a story retailed by J.H. Secretan:

> One day he sent for me to his office in Winnipeg and, rapidly revolving his chair, squinted at me over the top his pince-nez, at the same time unrolling a profile about one hundred miles at a time, saying, "Look here, some damned fool of an engineer has put in a tunnel up there, and I want you to go and *take it out*!" I asked if I might be permitted to see where the objectionable tunnel was. He kept rolling and unrolling the profile until he came to the fatal spike which showed a mud tunnel about 900 feet long — somewhere on the Bow River at mileage 942. I mildly suggested that the engineer, whoever he was, had not put the tunnel in for fun. He didn't care what the engineer did it for, but they were not going to build it and delay the rest of the work. "How long do you think it would take to build the cursed thing?" he asked. I guessed about twelve or fourteen months. That settled it. He was not there to build fool tunnels to please a lot of engineers. So, perfectly satisfied that the matter was settled and done with, he whirled around to his desk and went on with something else, simply remarking, "Mind you go up there *yourself* and a take that d–d tunnel out. Don't send anybody else."

> I asked for the profile, and when I reached the door, paused for a minute and said, "While I'm up there hadn't I better move some of the mountains back as I think they are too close to the river." The "old man" looked up for a second, said nothing, but I could see the generous proportions of his corporation shaking like a jelly. He was convulsed with laughter.

The prairie section of the CPR was not, as is so often thought, built across only flat plains. Its route also included low rolling hills that presented many obstacles to laying a well-graded railway line. These challenges, though, were nothing compared to those that had to be met laying track through the mountains of British Columbia and across the Canadian Shield. Van Horne's mettle and managerial genius were tested as never before in 1884 and 1885, the years in which the railway was pushed further in both these areas, to the west and the east.

Construction in mountainous British Columbia was especially challenging, for it was here that the most difficult terrain and weather along the entire CPR route were encountered. The seven-hundred-mile prairie section that lay between the Assiniboine River at Brandon, Manitoba, and the Elbow River at Calgary had required only one major structure — the South Saskatchewan Bridge at Medicine Hat. By contrast, the mountain line required many bridges, tunnels, and snow sheds, usually on the flanks of steep granite mountains pierced by deep canyons. Before construction in the mountains could be completed, miles of track had to be cut through solid rock and countless rivers had to be crossed, some by iron bridges more than a thousand feet in length and one by a wooden bridge two hundred and eighty-six feet above the water below — the highest bridge in North America. Moreover, fourteen streams had to be diverted from their natural beds by tunnelling them through solid rock.

Describing Van Horne's intervention in a Rocky Mountain canyon, an unidentified spectator, H.R. Lewis, wrote:

> There were men felling trees & men drafting great logs, men building trestles & braces & wooden bulwarks, men laboring to the utmost of their physical powers & men directing their labors, & one man there was, sturdy, plainly dressed & calm of bearing, who directed the directors. He seemed to be everywhere, giving his personal attention to each detail of the work. He found the spots claiming immediate attention & measured accurately with his eyes the speed of the rising waters.
>
> He superintended the unloading of rock brought by puffing engines & assisted with his own hands in placing the heavy blocks of stone. He told the carpenters how to secure the huge wooden braces, the smiths where to fasten their iron clamps & with it all never lost for one moment his cool, authoritative demeanor.

The horrendous construction problems posed by the mountain section frequently led even qualified engineers to disagree among themselves on how certain portions of the line should be built. On these occasions, Van Horne had to act as the final arbitrator on these "grave engineering questions." The fate of many workers rested on his decisions. Much of this difficult and dangerous toil was done by fifteen thousand Chinese labourers who were brought to British Columbia between 1880 and 1885 to work on the railway. Hundreds of them met their death as they built the line between Vancouver and Calgary, often from exposure in the harsh weather conditions or from being crushed by falling rock or killed by dynamite blasts.

To the east, the difficulties and costs associated with laying track across the six hundred and fifty-seven miles of remote, rugged terrain that lay between Callander and Port Arthur (now Thunder Bay), Ontario, presented a different type of challenge. Van Horne had no illusions about the magnitude of the problems involved in building in this region, particularly along the rocky stretch that hugs the shoreline of Lake Superior, which he himself defined as "two hundred miles of engineering impossibilities." However, exuding his usual confidence, he added, "But we'll bridge it."

The grading and track-laying crews began their work in 1883, starting out from both ends of Lake Superior. On this stretch of the route the crews had to deal with the extremely variable topography, the steep cliffs that descend to the lake, and the general lack of earth with which to construct embankments. Perhaps the greatest challenges were the many swampy muskegs — the crews had to re-lay one stretch of track seven times. There were sinkholes, too — seemingly solid patches of ground that suddenly gave way under the weight of a train, with costly, time-consuming results. And there were landslides — on one occasion a slide swept away a section of track and, with it, thousands of dollars' worth of steel rails. When the telegram conveying the bad news reached the unflappable Van Horne at this desk in Montreal, he merely lifted his eyebrows and uttered a quiet exclamation.

Construction was also hampered by the total lack of access to the northern shore of Lake Superior except over ice in the winter and by water during the rest of the year. Yet, somehow, steady supplies of the building materials had to get through. To this end, Van Horne ordered the purchase of boats to transport supplies and men to the north shore's work sites. He also ordered the construction of three twenty-three-hundred-ton steel passenger and cargo steamers. They were launched on Scotland's Clyde River and sailed across the Atlantic in October 1883. Eventually the boats were based in Owen Sound, where they became a vital link in the first-class immigrant services that the CPR was able to offer from Montreal to the Rockies in the summer.

It was during construction on the north shore that Van Horne imported the first "track-laying" machine to be used in Canada. It was his answer to the difficulties posed by track-laying, especially in challenging areas. A delivery gantry rather than an actual machine, it carried rails forward in troughs along one side of the lead car and ties on the other side.

Referring to Van Horne's multiple achievements on this stretch of the transcontinental, the authoritative *Railway and Shipping World* observed in 1900, "It is well to say in passing, that if Van Horne had accomplished nothing else, his victory over the engineering difficulties afforded by the line along Lake Superior's north shore would give him fame enough for one man."

Van Horne had to cope not only with the physical challenges that hampered the progress of construction, but also with labour shortages, strikes, and "the demon rum." In the West, which was under federal jurisdiction, the sale of alcohol was banned. It was not prohibited, however, in Ontario, where enterprising liquor peddlers found an eager market. Heading their list of customers were the toiling navvies, who frequently turned to alcohol

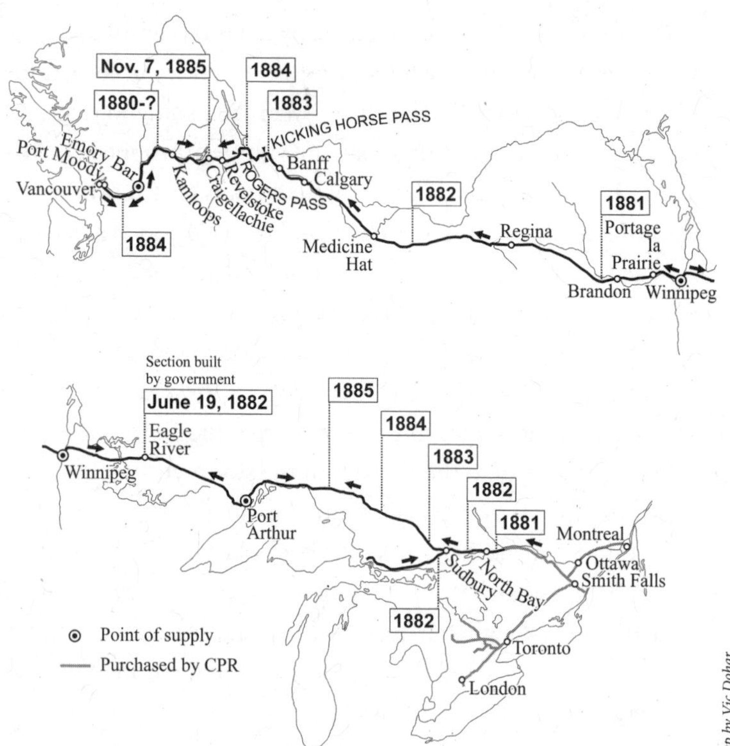

Construction of Canadian Pacific's main transcontinental line showing end of track at year's end.

for relief from the exhausting work they performed and the extremely primitive conditions under which they lived. Van Horne attempted to dampen rum's appeal by arranging for the construction crews to be well fed, but this solution was not enough to stave off a chronic liquor problem. All too often drunkenness led to lawlessness and violence, such as the rioting and gunplay that erupted on the north shore in October 1884. It was so serious that authorities summoned a magistrate and some policemen from Toronto to restore order.

Day-to-day problems such as these absorbed much of Van Horne's attention; but even as he was dealing with these concerns, he was spinning far-reaching plans for the CPR's future. He was convinced that the railway should strive to become an integrated international transportation company, with ships, grain elevators, hotels, and telegraph lines. And so the visionary Van Horne began to acquire ancillary services even as the main line was still being built. He arranged, for example, for the CPR to purchase control of a dormant express company, and he established the Canadian Pacific Telegraph service.

Knowing that the railway's economic survival depended on the successful settlement of the Prairies, he spearheaded the establishment of a wide-ranging and effective promotional scheme to attract settlers and tourists alike to the Northwest. The highlight of this campaign was an advertising program that saw the railway's immigration department distribute vast quantities of publicity material — posters, brochures, pamphlets — in the United States, Great Britain, and northern Europe. The hook to lure immigrants was Canada's huge agricultural potential. For tourists, the attention-grabber was Canada's natural wonders, particularly its mountains. A large coloured poster, produced as early as 1883, trumpets "The Grand Transcontinental Highway from the Cities of the East to Winnipeg and Manitoba's Boundless Wheatfields." The poster's bottom left-hand corner shows a clump of fresh produce and a vessel containing sheaves of wheat. Tourism was promoted by an article written by the Marquis of Lorne, Canada's former governor general, and reprinted as a pamphlet in 1886. Entitled "Our Railway to the Pacific," it is illustrated by engravings from drawings by the marquis's wife, Princess Louise. The pamphlet lavishes praise on the men who built the railway, the settlement opportunities it has opened up in the Canadian west, and Canada's scenic beauties.

Van Horne's longstanding interest in art meant that he took a special interest in the pictorial side of this project. In 1884, for example, Van Horne commissioned William Notman and Son, a well-known and highly respected Montreal photographic firm, to dispatch a party to the west to photograph the prairies and the construction of the CPR's line through the Rockies. He provided the photographer's son, William McFarlane Norman, with an official car for this purpose. Evidently the quality of the work and the grandeur of the photographed landscape met Van Horne's requirements exactly because a selection of the photos appeared in a pamphlet, *The Canadian Pacific: The New Highway to the East*. But nothing delighted Van Horne more than having the CPR sponsor artists to serve the cause, usually prominent Canadian landscape painters. His earliest recruit and the only artist actually commissioned by the CPR in these years was the English-born John Fraser. Among his works were black and white sketches used to promote tourism, one being a view of the Banff Springs Hotel. Non-commissioned artists also benefited from the CPR's largess. These artists were provided with free transportation after they convinced Van Horne that their work would serve the CPR's interests. Although copies of their paintings were used in promotional material, the originals often ended up in the private collections of Van Horne, George Stephen, and other company officials.

In 1884 Van Horne himself made a long-anticipated trip to British Columbia. He wanted to look over construction in the mountains and to decide on the location of the railway's Pacific terminus. Although Port Moody had been designated as the CPR's terminus, Van Horne and Stephen both had serious misgivings about its suitability as a port for the railway. In the spring of that year, for instance, he received news that Port Moody's harbour was too small for the CPR's purposes. Twelve miles further west, however, at Coal Harbour and False Creek (an extension of English Bay), there was a superb townsite. When he was finally able to set foot in Port Moody that August, Van Horne's fears about the location were confirmed. The next day, he travelled to the mouth of Burrard Inlet by boat. Here, just inside the inlet, he decided, would be the site of the new western terminus. After hard bargaining with the provincial government, the CPR agreed to extend the railway from Port Moody to Granville if the government gave the company half the peninsula on which the present city of Vancouver now sits. In addition to negotiating the formal agreement that resulted in 1885, Van Horne also named the townsite. He was always interested in sea captains, especially if they boasted Dutch blood, so he suggested that it be called "Vancouver" — after the island that had taken its name from George Vancouver, the intrepid explorer who had sailed off the B.C. coast in the eighteenth century.

George Stephen and the CPR directors and shareholders were all delighted with Van Horne's performance. At the annual shareholders' meeting on May 14, 1884, they elected him to the board of directors. Then, immediately after the meeting, the board elected him vice-president and appointed him to its executive committee. In less than two and a half years, Van Horne had progressed from being general manager of the railway's construction to a prestigious position and a member of its governing circle. But here he soon faced even greater challenges.

The Conservative government of John A. Macdonald thought that the CPR had been generously compensated by the transfer of existing rail lines to it, the land grant, and the tax and customs concessions. However, the extreme difficulties of building across the Canadian Shield and in British Columbia, in addition to the purchase of feeder lines in eastern Canada, soon led to huge cost overruns, and, by the summer of 1882, the company was in deep financial trouble.

To add to its misfortune, the CPR's enemies made vicious attempts to discredit it, thereby undermining the company's reputation in British and American financial circles. Foremost among the CPR's rivals was Van Horne's *bête noire*, the Grand Trunk Railway (GTR), a largely British-owned and -directed railway, whose main line ran from Sarnia and Toronto to Montreal. As early as 1873, Grand Trunk management tried to frustrate Sir Hugh Allan's attempts to generate loans in London, and, in the 1880s, they attacked the CPR on several fronts.

To raise much-needed funds, the CPR agreed to sell a huge chunk of its lands to an Anglo-Canadian consortium, the Northwest Land Company. This company was charged with managing town-site sales in several major western communities.

Still, the CPR edged ever closer to the financial abyss. In the fall of 1883, when the situation was critical, George Stephen decided to petition the federal government for relief. Previously Van Horne had left Stephen to scramble for money, but in November of that year he journeyed to Ottawa with Stephen and other CPR luminaries to make their case for additional funds. After arriving in the nation's capital, the mendicants went directly to Earnscliffe, the prime minister's home, to outline the situation to Macdonald and stress the absolute necessity of immediate government assistance.

Initially Macdonald turned them down. But he reversed his position after he heard John Henry Pope, the acting minister of railways and canals, declare, "The day the Canadian Pacific busts, the Conservative Party busts the day after." In other words, the fate of the Conservative Party was inextricably linked to that of the Canadian Pacific.

To provide the generous assistance demanded by Stephen, the Conservatives had to push a bill through Parliament that would grant the railway relief. For that to happen, however, they first had to examine the CPR's finances. Following a searching inquiry, the government engineer Collingwood Schreiber and the deputy minister of inland revenue reported that they were completely satisfied with the railway's accounts and integrity. Van Horne was then summoned to a Cabinet meeting to explain his company's progress and needs.

Meanwhile, the government took steps to provide immediate assistance to the CPR. Before the House of Commons met in January 1884, the Conservatives supported Stephen's application for an extension of a current loan from the Bank of Montreal, which had refused to grant one unless it had written assurance from the government that it stood by the Canadian Pacific for repayment of the loan. In addition, Stephen and the government also agreed at this time on the terms of aid sought by the CPR. For the company the stakes were enormous. As security for a huge loan, Stephen agreed to mortgage the entire railway, including land-grant bonds and outstanding stock. At Van Horne's instigation, Stephen also promised to have the main line completed in half the time stipulated in the original contract.

Late in the winter of 1883–84, Van Horne made another trip to Ottawa, this time to see history in the making. Here he watched the prelude to what would turn out to be one of the longest and most acrimonious debates in the history of the Canadian transcontinental railway. When the relief bill was presented to the House of Commons, it seemed that every agency and individual who opposed the CPR was given the opportunity to unite against it. Despite threatened defections within his own Cabinet and blistering attacks from outside, Macdonald nevertheless managed to push the relief bill through Parliament. He succeeded in doing so, however, only by resorting to considerable cajoling in caucus and behind the scenes and by awarding concessions to Quebec and the Maritimes. The bill finally became law on March 6, 1884. A week later the Bank of Montreal debt was retired.

Van Horne was taken aback and dismayed by all the frantic horse-trading and other political machinations required to keep the CPR afloat. To one Cabinet minister, he wrote, "It has always been a matter of principle with me never to enquire into a man's politics in transacting business, but I must say that our past winter's experience in Ottawa has somewhat staggered me." Hitherto, he had remained aloof from politics, whether in the United States or in Canada. He did not belong to any political party, and he repeatedly resisted the common Canadian practice of hiring staff on the basis of their political affiliation (to say nothing of religion). The only thing that mattered to Van Horne was individual ability. Nevertheless, he was prepared to play the political game if that was necessary to safeguard or further the CPR's interests. One such occasion arose during the 1883 Ontario provincial election, when Macdonald and the federal government asked for political assistance from the CPR. Acutely conscious of the railway's dependence on the government, Van Horne was quick to provide that support.

Regrettably, the government's generous loan did not spell an end to the railway's financial difficulties. In early 1885 Stephen found himself once again making frequent pilgrimages to Ottawa in the hope of obtaining even more financial assistance. While he haunted the anterooms of Cabinet members, Van Horne focused on cost-cutting, and Shaughnessy tried valiantly to stave off creditors. With bankruptcy once again a real possibility, what was needed was a dramatic event that would focus attention on the CPR's plight and underscore the vital role that could be played by a completed transcontinental railway. Fortunately, there was such an event — the North-West Rebellion, the second revolt led by Louis Riel, which broke out in March 1885.

For the first time in their history, Canadians were confronted by an armed uprising on their own soil with nothing but their own resources to defend themselves. Macdonald could have requested the assistance of imperial troops, but he rejected this option. Instead, he said, the government would use citizen soldiers — who, in all parts of the country, clamoured to enlist. Van Horne, recognizing a golden opportunity, lost no time in offering the use of the CPR to transport troops from eastern Canada to the Northwest. He insisted on but three conditions from the government; that they raise the troops, provide the CPR vice-president with a week's notice of their departure, and allow him free rein in making arrangements for their provisioning and transport.

In making his offer, Van Horne was fully aware of the good publicity that such a move would bring the railway. Indeed, he impressed on his subordinates that not only the CPR's reputation but perhaps its very existence would depend on the speed and efficiency with which it could transport men and equipment to the site of the uprising. He knew that there were still four breaks in the line north of Lake Superior, but he figured that sleighs could take the men over two of the gaps on the desolate frozen lake and that the troops could march over the other two. Regardless, even he must have felt somewhat apprehensive as he contemplated the challenge of shuttling men and military and artillery supplies over primitive, incomplete roads stretching across frozen, forested wasteland. Horrendous as the obstacles were, however, Van Horne, aided by Donald Smith and Joseph Wrigley, the Hudson's Bay Company trade commissioner, successfully resolved the problems associated with provisioning more than three thousand soldiers and transporting them, their horses, and their equipment over such distances.

In transporting troops quickly to the site of the insurrection, Fort Qu'Appelle, the CPR demonstrated its worth. No longer could the railway be regarded as a leech repeatedly sucking money from the federal treasury. Finally it was recognized as a real asset to the country, a steel rail binding the infant nation together. Van Horne soon detected the "very great change" in public opinion with respect to the need for the CPR, and he confidently predicted on April 4 that, "in the light of the present difficulty, Parliament will deal fairly with us before adjournment."

Parliament did eventually come to the company's aid, but not before the railway was almost pushed into bankruptcy by escalating costs and the chronic shortage of funds. The situation became especially critical in July 1885, when Van Horne was driving construction forward in British Columbia. Between July 14 and August 1, several CPR debts were slated to come due. This prospect, together with the knowledge that the pay car had not gone out in weeks, persuaded Van Horne to take immediate action. He ordered a special train to rush him to Ottawa on July 13, the day before the first note was due and while a relief bill was still being debated in the Senate. When he found

Macdonald, he informed him that the CPR would "go smash" the next day if Dominion Bridge called in its debt. The government had to do something fast. The prime minister could not hurry the Senate along in its deliberations, but that did not matter. Once the bridge company realized that Senate approval was imminent and that it would soon be paid, it gave the company a few days' grace. On July 20 the relief bill received royal assent, and a temporary loan of $5 million became available immediately. Three days later Stephen cabled from London that Baring Brothers, a well-known investment firm, would come to the CPR's rescue as well.

Henceforth Van Horne could banish financial worries from his mind and concentrate on pushing the line through to completion. As the eagerly awaited day fast approached, he was inundated with inquiries about the date and the place at which the final two rails would be joined. These inquiries were accompanied by a flood of requests for details about the ceremony that would be staged to mark the historic occasion.

Van Horne flirted briefly with the idea of organizing an elaborate ceremony, but he found it impossible to limit the number of invited guests. To do so would result in "a vast deal of disappointment and ill feeling," he informed a correspondent from Victoria. Furthermore, a big ceremony would have involved considerable expense — the last thing the company could afford. He therefore settled on the simple last-spike ceremony that unfolded that raw November day at Craigellachie, British Columbia.

6

Headed for the Top

After the low-key ceremony that marked the completion of Canada's transcontinental railway, William Van Horne, his son Bennie, and other members of the official party with their guests scrambled aboard their special train. It then set off for Port Moody, winding its way along the Thompson River Valley and down the scenic Fraser Canyon to the Pacific port. There they boarded the steamer *Princess Louise*, which took them for a sail around beautiful Burrard Inlet and English Bay. Then they crossed to Vancouver Island for a round of congratulatory speeches in Victoria, the capital of British Columbia. Finally they returned to the mainland, where they climbed aboard the special train headed for Winnipeg.

But amid all this solemnity, Van Horne could not resist an elaborate practical joke. It centred on Donald Smith, the man who had driven the iconic last spike just the week before and who owned several residences in Canada. One of these properties,

Silver Heights, was located a few miles west of Winnipeg, and here Smith kept a herd of Aberdeen cattle. Van Horne had arranged for a party to be staged in the then unoccupied house on the estate. He had a spur line built from Winnipeg to the residence, hired cooks and domestic helpers, and ordered vast quantities of the best food and drinks. Close to noon on November 15, when the special train entered the spur, the party was deep in conversation, and Smith did not notice that the engineer had reversed the engine. Then, suddenly, he spotted "a very neat place" and some fine Aberdeen cattle. "This is really very strange," he said, puzzled, and, when the house came into view, he thought he was truly going crazy: he had never seen another place "so exactly like Silver Heights." At this point his companions all burst out laughing — and Smith, glancing outside, began to laugh too. Van Horne's imaginative practical joke had stuck just the right note for the occasion.

Another milestone for the CPR arrived on June 28, 1886, when the first transcontinental passenger train departed from Montreal bound for the Pacific coast. Anticipating the day when bales of silk would soon be arriving from China and Japan, the city fathers hung silken banners on the engine and ordered a fifteen-gun salute. As the smoke-belching train drew slowly out of Dalhousie Square station, bound for Port Moody, Van Horne heard the guns of the Montreal battery boom and the loud cheers of the assembled crowd echo around him.

Already, however, Van Horne knew that massive repairs were needed on many sections of the trans-Canada railway. In June 1885 George Stephen had confidently told the CPR shareholders that the CPR's main line would be completed and in perfect condition by the spring of 1886 — that it would exceed the standards fixed in its contract with the government. But construction had proceeded so rapidly that the company had resorted to using many temporary structures. Whenever Van Horne went out on the line, he realized that it had been merely slapped down in places and that, for hundreds of miles, it consisted of little more than ties and the two rails that lay across them with a row of telegraph poles along one side. On the Prairies the line had little or no ballast, and in more rugged country, particularly in the western mountains, it skirted many minor obstructions instead of barrelling through them. North America's first true transcontinental railway was therefore crooked in places and full of curves. To further complicate matters, the railway trestles that had been built of timber instead of masonry or iron were so rickety that trains had to crawl across them. Moreover, many a station, loading dock, or warehouse also needed to be rebuilt or enlarged.

Van Horne therefore had to set to work immediately to supervise the huge task of rebuilding long stretches of the line. Since this required additional money, he had to lobby for funds from a disgruntled government to complete the work. He also had to wrestle with the fallout from disputes and litigation with contractors on the Lake Superior section, and with the government on the rugged Fraser Canyon section that had been built by the American contractor Andrew Onderdonk.

As always, countless little details that related peripherally to the running of a railway competed for his attention. There was a steady stream of inquiries about employment opportunities and a barrage of requests for free passes. Notable among these were endearing queries from Father Albert Lacombe, who sought reduced fares and the use of a car for a priests' excursion. Van Horne had first met the renowned missionary to the

Blackfoot Indians at Rat Portage, when the rugged priest was attending to the spiritual needs of hundreds of drinking, blaspheming, fighting railway construction workers. This first meeting with Lacombe made a profound and lasting impression on Van Horne. Later, both he and the CPR would owe a huge debt of gratitude to "his special friend" for doing much to ease relations between the Blackfoot and the company during construction on the Prairies. Of course his requests had to be granted.

One excursion stood out above all the others for Van Horne — the journey taken in July 1886 by Sir John A. Macdonald and his formidable wife, Agnes, to the West. Pressure of business had prevented the prime minister from travelling on the first scheduled transcontinental train trip, and this one would be the only visit he ever made to the Great West. Van Horne provided the best, as he outfitted a private car for Sir John's party with fine-meshed window screens to keep out the dust and the mosquitoes. He also arranged for most of the travelling to be done by night to allow the honoured guests ample time for rest and the opportunity to see scenery along the entire line by daylight. Lady Macdonald made the most of it, as she rode on the exposed locomotive cowcatcher for almost all the journey between Canmore, Alberta, and Port Moody — a distance of nearly six hundred miles.

That same July, Van Horne embarked on the first of his annual inspection tours from Montreal to the West coast. Usually he was accompanied by a few CPR co-directors and personal friends, and occasionally by Bennie and other family members. These trips became noted for their good company and good cheer, much of it supplied by Van Horne himself. He often treated his guests to boyish practical jokes, assisted by Jimmy French, his incomparable black porter. A short, thickset man with a highly mobile face and a quick wit, French was devoted to the CPR, Van Horne, and his family. When Addie was ill in 1891, for instance, he repeatedly visited their Montreal home to inquire about her health and to recommend a reviving trip under his care in the *Saskatchewan* — Van Horne's private car.

Once the transcontinental railway was constructed, George Stephen focused almost exclusively on financing and large policy questions, and he left the day-to-day management of the CPR to his vice-president, Van Horne. With full operational control, Van Horne turned most of his attention to developing traffic, for only if there was sufficient freight and passenger business could the railway earn enough to meet its staggering financial charges. In the next few years he diversified the company's operations by acquiring grain elevators, flour mills, express and telegraph operations, port facilities, maritime fleets, agricultural and timber lands, and numerous tourist services, including hotels. In terms of actual rail operations, he not only continued the policy of acquiring a network of rail lines in the settled industrial regions of eastern Canada, but he also strove to develop rail links to established markets in New England and the American Midwest.

In the grand vision entertained by Van Horne and George Stephen, the CPR was more than just the first pan-Canadian corporation — it was part of an integrated transportation network that would girdle the globe. "Canada is doing business on a back street," Van Horne once observed. "We must put her on a thoroughfare."

To put the CPR on a thoroughfare, he arranged for the company to operate steamships on both the Pacific and the Atlantic coasts. In 1886 the company presented a formal tender to the British government to provide a first-class, subsidized mail service between Hong Kong and Vancouver: it would charter steamships for the following year and use its own ships in 1888. After long and complicated negotiations between the CPR and the British and Canadian governments, the company finally won a formal contract for the mail service. No sooner was this done than the CPR ordered three liners in 1889 to maintain the monthly service — the *Empress of India*, *Empress of Japan*, and *Empress of China*. Van Horne named all three vessels, choosing the designation "Empress" to reflect the ships' superiority over all anticipated competition. He also designed the red and white checker-board house flag that was flown on all Canadian Pacific ships for the next eighty years. Efficient to operate, mechanically sound, aesthetically pleasing, and well upholstered, these vessels earned a reputation that other lines found difficult to equal.

Van Horne swelled with pride on April 28, 1891, when the graceful, clipper-bowed *Empress of India* docked in Vancouver. The first of the majestic Empress liners to be completed, she had sailed from Liverpool for the Pacific by way of the Suez Canal. More than a hundred first-class passengers had booked passage for what would be the closest thing to a world cruise that had yet been offered. When the liner docked at Vancouver, Van Horne and some of the company directors were on hand to welcome her. As part of the welcoming ceremonies, a grand banquet and ball were staged at the Hotel Vancouver. However, since Van Horne disliked large, formal functions, he departed for Montreal that very afternoon.

In these same years, Van Horne hired New York society architect Bruce Price, who had designed Montreal's Windsor Station, to design the Banff Springs Hotel and Quebec City's Château Frontenac. The CPR's vice-president also immersed himself in immigration schemes, continued to sponsor artists and photographers to capture CPR landmarks, and invented numerous catchy slogans to lure tourists to Canada. The picturesque mountain hotels designed by Price and Thomas Sorby were all part of Van Horne's grand scheme to generate traffic for the railway and to make the line's costly mountain section pay for itself. "Since we can't export the scenery, we'll have to import the tourists," he reportedly said as he contemplated the stunning mountain views. He advertised the Rockies as "1001 Switzerlands Rolled into One." And, to attract tourists to this part of the world, he set out to provide first-class travellers with excellent ship and train service and superior hotels that commanded the choicest mountain views.

Banff Springs Hotel, the most celebrated of the CPR's mountain hostelries, owed its construction indirectly to the discovery of several natural hot springs on the flanks of Sulphur Mountain. Van Horne visited the springs early in 1885 and immediately sized up their tourist potential: "These springs," he said, "are worth a million dollars." He decided to build a top-notch hotel near the springs, at the confluence of the Bow and Spray Rivers, and instructed Bruce Price to draw up the plans. But the construction met with one conspicuous mishap. When Van Horne visited the building site in the summer of 1887, he was outraged to see that the contractor had oriented the hotel backwards, thereby providing the kitchens with the best view of the mountain ranges and the valley below. One colleague observed: "Van Horne was one of the most considerate and even-tempered of men, but when an explosion came it was magnificent." Fortunately, the solution was simple: Van Horne called for a sheet of paper, sketched a rotunda pavilion on the spot, and directed that it be situated to provide hotel guests with a magnificent view.

When the hotel was completed in the spring of 1888, Van Horne boasted that it was the "Finest Hotel on the North American Continent." Soon it welcomed the first of the thousands of tourists who would visit it each year. But the Banff Springs Hotel also performed another, more significant role: it initiated the "chateau style" that came to characterize many of the hotels erected by the CPR and other railways, as well as railway stations and apartment complexes. Even several large government buildings in Ottawa adopted this style.

It is impossible to know how much Van Horne contributed to the design of the Banff Springs Hotel and Windsor Station, the CPR's principal terminal and administrative headquarters, but he did make a considerable contribution to Quebec City's Château Frontenac. Van Horne watched over every stage of this hotel's design, and he even took Bruce Price out in a small boat on the St. Lawrence River one day to make sure that the elevation of the building's imposing round tower was "sufficiently majestic."

Van Horne's architectural flair was also put to good use designing the prototype for the quaint CPR log stations that soon became famous in the mountains of British Columbia. When CPR officials could not decide what should replace the boxcar that had been serving as a primitive station at Banff, Van Horne discussed the problems with officials at the site. Then he grabbed a sheet of paper, sketched a log chalet, and, gesturing in the direction of the mountain slopes, announced: "Lots of good logs there. Cut them, peel them, and build your station."

Van Horne also commissioned artists to produce paintings to hang in company hotels and in the private collections of CPR directors. In an unusual promotional scheme, he offered artists free transportation and accommodation to paint the magnificent scenery along the CPR line that pierced the Rockies and the

Selkirk Mountains. In the summer of 1889 he dispatched the well-known American painter Albert Bierstadt and several other artists to the West, instructing them to paint large oil canvases of designated landmarks. On behalf of his colleague George Stephen, he asked Bierstadt to produce a large painting of Mount Baker — and told him the precise vantage point from which to paint it. He then judged the final product, even though Bierstadt was one of the most respected of all Rocky Mountain landscape painters, and Stephen was a connoisseur and patron of fine art.

Another artist recruited by Van Horne was John Hammond, who journeyed west to Asia to promote the newly inaugurated connections that enabled CPR steamships from Vancouver to meet P & O liners from the Orient. By this means, English and European tourists could travel around the world, with the CPR furnishing the needed link. Hammond toured the Japanese countryside, sketching scenes for paintings that were designed to entice tourists to the Far East.

Not surprisingly, Van Horne threw himself into the CPR's wide-ranging promotional campaign to attract settlers to the Prairie West. At the time, Maritimers and Quebecers were still pouring into the New England states in search of jobs, and Van Horne set out to persuade them to settle instead in Canada's Northwest Territory. He even appointed priests as colonizing agents to encourage the recruitment of French Canadians who were already toiling in factories across the border. He loved to compose catchy slogans to capture people's attention. When the company's passenger service was inaugurated, people in Montreal, Toronto, and other large centres were puzzled and astonished one morning to see billboards featuring the word "Parisien Politeness on the CPR," "Wise Men of the East Go West on the CPR," and other such jingles.

The Canada Northwest Land Company was established earlier as part of the land-settlement campaign, and Van Horne served for years as its president. He had his own pronounced views on land settlement. Central to his thinking was the belief that homesteaders should be grouped in settlements and not be separated from each other by large, unoccupied spaces. "You have no doubt observed," he wrote his friend Rudyard Kipling, who had probably met Van Horne on one of his trips to England, "that the largest buildings in the new western states and in western Canada are usually large insane asylums." Isolation, he told the famous writer and Imperialist, had contributed more than any other factor to filling these buildings. For the man who was "out all day busy with his work," isolation did not present a major problem, but it did to "the woman who eats out her soul in loneliness." He urged the Canadian government to change its surveying system in the Northwest. Rather than the block pattern it favoured, the government, he said, should provide for triangular farms that radiated out from small centres of settlement. These centres, in turn, should be clustered around a larger village and be connected by roads. The government, however, rejected his farsighted suggestion.

In addition to all his other responsibilities, Van Horne was also involved in litigation relating to the section of the railway, built for the government by Andrew Onderdonk, which extended from Port Moody through the Fraser Canyon to Savona's Ferry at the western end of Lake Kamloops. Neither George Stephen nor Van Horne believed that this part of the line had been soundly constructed. After inspecting the section in 1886, they concluded that only extensive and hugely expensive reworking would bring the line up to standard.

But who would be liable for this repair, estimated to be as high as $12 million? Opposing this view was John Henry Pope, the minister of railways and canals when this particular stretch was constructed. Pope was convinced that the work had been well done and, when he stood his ground, the stage was set for a protracted feud between him and Van Horne. Relations between the men became especially bitter in 1887, when the CPR launched a multimillion dollar claim against the government. In its claim, the company contended that the disputed section did not measure up to the required standards outlined in the Act of 1881. But the hard-working, conscientious Pope was convinced that he was right, and he dismissed the Canadian Pacific's claim. It was, he said, merely a scheme on the part of Van Horne and his associates to extort even more money from the government.

Eventually both parties agreed to arbitration, and, although the arbitrators began their sittings in February 1888, they did not get an agreement for more than three years. During that investigation, arbitration counsel and witnesses spent weeks at a time along the disputed portion of the line. Van Horne was the chief witness and, in late June 1888, he journeyed west to Vancouver, where the court's sessions continued day after day in the Hotel Vancouver. There he was subject to searching cross-examination by the leading legal figures of the day. As he delivered his opinion of the contested work he was characteristically blunt, if not reckless. His assessment led one of the arbitrators to remark out of court that, if one-half of what Van Horne said was true, the company ought to stop operating the line immediately. Collingwood Schreiber, the engineer-in-chief to the federal government, went so far as to tell Pope that, by trashing the government construction and claiming that the section was dangerous, Van Horne had placed himself in an untenable position. Given that he had not taken a single precaution against accidents, "should an accident occur, he would find it difficult to keep outside the walls of the Penitentiary."

However, the greatest demand on Van Horne's attention in these years was the agitation in Manitoba for "free-for-all" railway construction. At the root of this discontent was the monopoly clause in the CPR's charter: it forbade other federally chartered companies from building south of the CPR's main line, except in a southwest direction, and even then no competing line was to come within fifteen miles of the international border. Manitobans protested vigorously against this clause, goaded by their fear of monopolies and high freight rates and their growing sense of alienation from eastern Canada.

After the federal government disallowed three acts intended by the Manitoba government to encourage local railway construction, a storm of indignation swept across the province. Meetings were convened everywhere to protest against the perceived outrage and to draw up plans to prevent any repetition of it.

By 1887 Manitoba had become a hotbed of disallowance agitation and railway plotting. In the resulting turmoil, George Stephen and William Van Horne became, for Winnipeggers, the two most unpopular men in Canada. Van Horne retorted that, when the citizens decided to burn them in effigy, they would need one mattress for Sir George, but two to do justice to him! Finally, in April 1888, legislation was presented to the House of Commons to do away with the monopoly clause. But Van Horne still got his revenge — in the "Battle of Fort Whyte."

In 1888 the Northern Pacific Railroad set out to lay its Portage la Prairie line, known as the Northern Pacific and Manitoba Railway. Some fifteen miles west of Winnipeg, its tracks were poised to cross those of a CPR branch line, deep in the heart of CPR territory. The Northern Pacific and Manitoba laid its track up to the CPR branch line, installed a diamond crossing, and then continued on its way — all in the dead of night. The next day, CPR men ripped out the crossing. An infuriated Van Horne instructed his western superintendent, William Whyte, to take appropriate action. In the middle of the following night, an old CPR engine was ditched at the crossing point and some two hundred and fifty men from the CPR's Winnipeg shops were summoned to prevent its removal. Soon swarms of Northern Pacific workers showed up and, for five days, insults were traded back and forth. They did not cease until the Manitoba government called out the militia and had three hundred special constables sworn in specifically to lay the crossing, by force if necessary. With this action, bloodshed was averted.

The issue was finally left to the Supreme Court of Canada to decide. Its ruling, delivered that December, was in favour of the Northern Pacific and Manitoba. The combatants dispersed, the track was laid, and the diamond was reinstalled. The CPR had surrendered, but Van Horne's reckless actions constituted a public relations disaster for the railway. Whatever meagre support it had left in Manitoba quickly vanished.

By this time, however, Van Horne was president of the Canadian Pacific Railway. On April 7, 1888, he was unanimously elected to the position at a meeting of the board of directors in Montreal. George Stephen, who had resigned from the position after seven years of almost constant anxiety and struggle, deemed it right that somebody experienced in railway administration should take his place.

Before leaving for a holiday in England in September 1889, Stephen went to great pains to smooth the way for Van Horne in his dealings with the prime minister. In a letter to Macdonald, he wrote:

> You may be sure of one thing, Van Horne wants nothing from the Government that he is not on every ground justified in asking. You are quite "safe" in giving him your whole confidence. I know him better, perhaps, than anyone here and I am satisfied that I make no mistake when I ask you to trust him and to dismiss from your mind all suspicion that would lead you to look upon him as a sharper bound to take advantage of the Government every time he gets the chance.

Then, after Stephen retired in England, he dispatched a steady stream of letters to his successor. Van Horne in turn used him as a sounding board and the CPR's direct link to the British financial markets. He took care to keep Stephen abreast of CPR developments in frequent telegrams and letters. Strangely, despite their long and close association, these communications were written in a surprisingly formal style. Stephen continued to serve as a CPR director and member of the executive committee until his resignation in 1893.

After he became president of the CPR, Van Horne had the continuing support of able and hard-working colleagues. The most important of these men was the assistant general manager, Thomas G. Shaughnessy. His love of minutiae, talent for administration, and acumen for business had been abundantly demonstrated over

Courtesy of Library and Archives Canada, PA207269.

George Stephen (later Lord Mount Stephen). The Scottish-born financier was the first president of the Canadian Pacific Railway, in which capacity he became a good friend of Van Horne.

the years, and Van Horne would continue to depend on him. In fact, he appointed Shaughnessy assistant to the president in 1889.

As president, Van Horne received a substantial boost in salary — from $30,000 to $50,000 per annum, retroactive to the beginning of the year. His new title did not, however, increase his responsibilities in any way. He was already in full control of company operations — and had been for years. Still, the announcement of his new appointment must have filled him with pride. After all, at the comparatively young age of forty-five, he had become the president of a railway system that comprised over five thousand miles of line, owned 14 million acres of land, and boasted assets of $189 million. Moreover, because of the connections it had forged with American lines and with China, Japan, and the Maritime provinces (through the Short

Line, which, when completed, would link Montreal with the Maritimes), the CPR was indeed a global transportation system. As such, it afforded unlimited challenges for the ever-ambitious and creative Van Horne, who now occupied the leading post in the Canadian railroading world.

7

Czar of the CPR

In the eleven years that he presided at the helm of the CPR (1888–99), Van Horne strove mightily to expand the company by both construction and acquisitions. A new railway had to grow, he argued, if it was to avoid being swallowed up by a competing railway or, worse, going bankrupt. This belief was reinforced by the experience he had acquired in managing American railways during a period of great consolidation. Unfortunately, when Van Horne served as the CPR's president, Canada was gripped by a prolonged depression for most of the time. As a result, he was forced to tone down expansion and, when the depression reached its lowest point in 1894, he had to introduce stringent economy measures.

This growth was not always straightforward and painless, however, especially for the piecemeal assembly of the Short Line, which ran from Montreal through central Maine to Saint

John, New Brunswick. George Stephen had earlier flirted with the idea of making Portland, Maine, a destination for the CPR because he wanted the railway to obtain an Atlantic steamship connection — and that required a port that was ice free in the winter. The choice of Portland raised such a storm of protest in New Brunswick and Nova Scotia, however, that the idea had to be abandoned in favour of a Canadian port. The distance from Montreal to the Atlantic coast could be reduced significantly, the Maritimers pointed out, if a railway were built eastward across the central part of Maine — and so it came to be called the Short Line. To encourage the construction of such a line, Parliament approved a cash subsidy for it in 1884. As an additional inducement, Macdonald assured Stephen that the government-owned Intercolonial Railway would provide running rights over its line from Saint John to Halifax. Moreover, through traffic between Montreal and Nova Scotia / New Brunswick would be routed over the Short Line, and the Intercolonial would be operated principally as a local railway. The CPR, therefore, faced mounting pressure to take over the project. Eventually it did, though Van Horne and George Stephen always insisted that the CPR did so only with great reluctance. Even before the line was completed in June 1889, these two men had cause to regret that the CPR ever became involved in the enterprise because of the heavy financial obligations it imposed. Moreover, once the new line opened for traffic, the Intercolonial Railway, instead of cooperating with the CPR, treated it as a competitor.

These problems caused Van Horne great distress. Frustrated beyond words, he deluged Prime Minister Macdonald with letters about the troublesome railway: "This is far from the treatment that the Company had reason to expect when it undertook the building of the 'Short Line,'" he exploded in a letter to

Sir John A. Macdonald in July 1889, only one month after the line began operating. "Nearly nine millions are now invested in that line which such an attitude on the part of the officers of the Intercolonial Railway will make absolutely valueless, or worse than valueless." And in October of that same year, he declared, "The CPR has been grievously wronged."

In Ontario, CPR expansion continued to rouse the ire of its long-time antagonist, the Grand Trunk Railway. In their attempts to harmonize their expansion plans and execute them smoothly, Van Horne and Joseph Hickson, the GTR's forceful general manager, both had to make concessions. These compromises required them to meet face to face in sometimes gruelling negotiations. In one such session, two months before Van Horne assumed the CPR presidency, the two men begged, cajoled, bluffed, and argued for four hours. Another round so exasperated Van Horne that he forwarded a copy of a letter from Hickson to George Stephen, fuming: "It has been a repetition of the old story — carrying on the negotiations up to the very last minute and then raising a new point relating to an outside matter."

Notwithstanding the prolonged depression, the CPR spent huge sums of money during Van Horne's presidency to improve its main line and to build or acquire branch lines linking it to parts of Manitoba and the northern prairies. Thanks to these expenditures and to links forged in southwestern Ontario and the Atlantic, the basic system was complete by 1890.

Expansion in the United States led, not surprisingly, to a renewal of clashes with Van Horne's old friend and railroading rival, James Jerome Hill. Their rivalry reached new heights after the CPR snapped up the Minneapolis, St. Paul & Sault Ste. Marie Railroad, commonly referred to as the Soo Line, along with another small railway, the Duluth, South Shore and Atlantic.

Even before these acquisitions, Van Horne's company was taking westbound freight in the American East and Midwest from American carriers bound for San Francisco. After the acquisition of these lines, the rivalry between the Great Northern, Hill's celebrated railway, and the CPR increased. It became even more intense after Van Horne scooped up the Duluth and Winnipeg, which the CPR would later surrender to Hill. However, even after the CPR gave up this company, its Soo Line harassed the Great Northern mercilessly. This encroachment prompted Hill to turn his attention to the West. Soon he built Great Northern branch lines northward towards the British Columbia border, angling for the rich coal deposits in the Crows Nest Pass area. Van Horne was furious. Looking at a map of British Columbia that showed the approaching lines, he bellowed at an engineer, "Look at these … like hungry hounds ready to jump in!"

The problem of international railway relations in the Northwest could have been resolved by a contract that divided traffic equitably between Hill's railway and the CPR. Neither side, though, was prepared to cooperate. As a result, the struggle between the two companies — and between Van Horne and Hill — continued throughout the 1890s. Ironically, Van Horne and Hill, by their own admission, admired each other. In their personal dealings, they would exchange passes, visit each other's railways, call on each other in their homes, and swap news about their latest art purchases. But when it came to operating rival railway systems, the two dynamos engaged in fierce, bare-knuckled competition. Contemplating the looming struggle with the Great Northern, Van Horne remarked in 1892 to Thomas Skinner, a London financier and CPR director: "I think just as much of Mr. Hill personally as it is possible for me to think of anybody who is opposed to the Canadian Pacific, but I would rather see him hung, drawn and quartered rather than have the Canadian Pacific lose ten cents through his Great Northern Railway." Given the tensions of bitter competition, it is a wonder that their mutual regard for each other managed to survive — but survive it did.

James Hill was not Van Horne's only American foe in the ruthless railway expansion game. In pressing his competitive edge so fiercely, the CPR president also attracted the hostility of other American railways — those companies that felt threatened by the CPR's success in forging strategic American connections. Van Horne's acquisition of the Soo Line and the Duluth, South Shore and Atlantic crystallized much of this opposition. Indeed, it stirred up the agitation so effectively that, in 1889, the U.S. Senate's Interstate Commerce Committee embarked on a study of Canadian railway operations in the United States.

In an effort to quell the opposition, Van Horne engaged an American lawyer to look after CPR interests in Washington, and he himself journeyed to the American capital to present his company's case. Ultimately, the Senate committee made only one recommendation relating to railways. As a result, and because of the failure of the U.S. Congress to take decisive steps regarding Canadian competition, American agitation persisted for years. In the face of one particular storm, Van Horne even arranged for the Canadian Pacific's case to be presented directly to President Benjamin Harrison, who had been threatening to issue a proclamation against Canadian railways. Fortunately, the president finally withdrew his threat. George Stephen was quick to commiserate with Van Horne, writing in January 1893: "It is very satisfactory to find that your record is so clear and clean. It is very annoying and trying to be obliged to suffer from grumbles and unfair interpretations."

Railway competitors were not the only antagonists that Van Horne had to deal with in these years. He also had to confront the organizers of a railway strike that erupted in 1892 over wages. On this occasion, as in previous strikes, he revealed his anti-union prejudices. In the ensuing struggle, the CPR employed strike breakers, hired special police to guard its property, and had auxiliary police sworn in by cooperative police magistrates in almost every major centre the company served. On March 21, 1892, Van Horne and Thomas Shaughnessy — now vice-president of the CPR — raised the ante still further. They ordered company officials to administer a loyalty oath to workers in the CPR's Eastern Division. This demand decided the issue for the men in northern Ontario, who, despite having no previous grievances against the company, voted to go out on strike. As a result, Van Horne and other CPR officials awoke on March 22 to the news that another seven hundred and fifty-two miles of track had been tied up. Faced with this setback, the company capitulated. On March 23, Van Horne ratified an agreement that represented an outstanding victory for the unionists. He had reluctantly, but pragmatically, concluded that further resistance would be drawn out and costly.

Van Horne was in the prime of life in 1894. Fifty-one years of age, he had put on weight over the years. The stocky body of youth had yielded to spreading girth, the result of too many hours at his desk, lack of exercise, and a gargantuan appetite. The receding hairline had long since been replaced by a bald pate, and his clipped beard was now flecked with grey. In fact, he bore a striking resemblance to the third Marquis of Salisbury, who was then Britain's prime minister.

Notwithstanding the signs of middle age, Van Horne continued to be a high-voltage dynamo, driven by ambition and determination. He still toiled incredibly long hours, whether at his desk or rushing across the continent. But his body, which he had abused so often, had begun to register the occasional protest. In 1894 he experienced the first of them — a prolonged attack of bronchitis that threatened to take up "permanent quarters" if he did not escape to a warmer climate. In the hope of regaining his health, Van Horne left Montreal on December 5 for England and the Continent. He planned to be away for five or six weeks.

During his brief sojourn in England, he visited his friend Robert Horne-Payne, a financial genius who was frequently called upon to handle loans for Canadian railways. Before leaving rain-soaked London for the Continent, Van Horne also met with his old colleague and friend George Stephen. Unfortunately, the former CPR president was worried by this meeting, and he later wrote an alarming letter to Shaughnessy:

> It is quite evident that Sir William, either from failing health or from allowing other things to occupy his mind, is no longer able to give the affairs of the company his undivided attention. His want of grasp and knowledge of the true position of the Company was, painfully, twice shown at our conference on Tuesday last, and can only be explained on the assumption that he had never given his mind to the matter.... His actions gave me the impression that he felt like a man who knew he was in a mess and had not the usual courage to look his position in the face. His apparent indifference and inability to

> realize the gravity of the position I can account for in no other way.
>
> From what I have thus said, you will see that all my confidence in the ability of Sir William to save the Company has gone, and it is to you alone that I look, if disaster is to be avoided.

In Paris, the weather may have been raw and wet, but at least Van Horne could visit the Louvre, hobnob with art dealers, and dine with friends at the famous restaurant Joseph's. There, "the most famous cook in the world" attended to him and his party in person. The weather continued to disappoint in Italy. In a desperate search for warmth, Van Horne persevered through a snowstorm to Naples and travelled on to Sorrento, the seaside resort across the bay from Naples. Notwithstanding the bitter cold, Van Horne was so captivated by Sorrento's picturesque charm that he admitted in a letter to Addie that he liked Italy and its people. "Both are better than I expected," he wrote.

Addie, meanwhile, was holding the fort in frigid Montreal. There she had to contend with Governor General Lord Aberdeen and his entourage, who arrived on her doorstep shortly after her husband's departure for Europe. Although accustomed to orchestrating countless dinners and weekends for all manner of guests, Addie at times rebelled openly against the role of dutiful wife. And this was one such occasion. In a letter to Van Horne, she let her pent-up frustration boil over. "I am sorry that you could not see more of London. How I wish you could go once & not be obliged to meet 'High Commissioners' & others on business. Let us plan to enjoy life a little before we get too old or infirm. We are always waiting on other people & I am tired of it."

In May 1894, Lord Aberdeen informed Van Horne that an honorary knighthood could be his for the taking — the third time he had been offered this honour. Previously, in 1891 and 1892, he had turned down Queen Victoria's proposal. Explaining his refusal in 1892, Van Horne told Prime Minister Sir John Abbott that he felt it would be a great mistake for him to accept a knighthood in the near future. He had reached this conclusion after considering several factors, "the chief one being the probability of renewed attacks on the CPR in the United States." He would not, he said, countenance any honour that might cost the CPR "an ounce of advantage." Nevertheless, when the offer was made the third time, almost six years after he had become a naturalized British subject, Van Horne accepted it. As a result, the Queen's birthday list of honours in May 1894 announced his appointment as an Honorary Knight Commander of the order of St. Michael and St. George.

Van Horne was at first uncomfortable with his new title. Walking to his Windsor Station office on the morning his knighthood was announced, he was repeatedly accosted by friends and acquaintances offering hearty congratulations. When his elderly office attendant, who for years had greeted him with a friendly salute, now made a servile bow and intoned, "Good morning, Sir William!" Van Horne could only mutter, "Oh Hell," and beat a hasty retreat.

Not surprisingly, Van Horne's acceptance of a knighthood buttressed a widely held belief that he had lost all love for his native country, the United States, and had become one of its most intractable opponents. This attitude riled the railway magnate, and he went to great lengths to squelch the idea and make it clear that, when he acted against American interests, it was simply because of his loyalty to the CPR. When the vehemently anti-CPR

New York *Sun* described him as "originally an American but now a fierce Tory hater of all things American," he dispatched a bristling letter of protest to the editor.

Canada was still in the grip of the depression when Van Horne returned to Montreal from his Mediterranean vacation in January 1895. Although relieved to be cured of his bronchitis, he felt only dismay and anxiety as he contemplated the trials now confronting him. The economic climate was so grim that, in February, Stephen dispatched a coded cablegram to Van Horne suggesting that the CPR suspend payment on its proposed dividend.

For some reason — perhaps because he had lost all faith in Van Horne's management or because he wanted to advance the interests of the Great Northern, with which he was still associated, or for both — Stephen also began advising CPR shareholders to sell their shares. He was joined in undermining confidence in the railway by Thomas Skinner, who was also supposedly a friend of Van Horne. Their comments seemed to support wild rumours that were circulating about certain actions by company directors, and, as a result, CPR shares plummeted to an all-time low. They would have skidded even lower but for some German capitalists, who, advised by Van Horne's friend Adolph Boissevain, a Dutch financier, purchased a large number of shares. Fortunately, by the fall of 1895, business had recovered. The following year, gross and net earnings had almost returned to their 1892 levels. The CPR had reeled under the weight of hard times, but it had not collapsed. It had weathered the storm and, just as Van Horne had foreseen, would soon return to profitability.

The return of the CPR to financial prosperity helped to improve Van Horne's outlook on life. So, surprisingly, did the federal Liberal Party's accession to power in 1896. Given his past performance, Van Horne might have been expected to intervene directly in this campaign, but he did not. In the 1891 federal campaign, when reciprocity with the United States was the Liberal Party's central plank, Van Horne had vehemently denounced this policy to end the protection of Canadian industries and introduce free trade. Unrestricted reciprocity would bring "prostration and ruin" to Canada, he wrote to Conservative Senator G.A. Dandurand. Much to Van Horne's horror, the letter was later printed in the Montreal *Gazette*. The CPR president considered damage control, but Shaughnessy immediately shot down this suggestion. The company had already been tarred with a political brush, he argued, and it should now give all the assistance it could to the Conservatives, who opposed reciprocity. In his own personal politics, Van Horne had always leaned towards the Conservatives, and he and Shaughnessy now set about throwing the massive weight of the CPR and its purse behind the party.

In the 1896 contest, by contrast, Van Horne and the CPR remained on the sidelines. Nevertheless, observers found it difficult to believe his repeated denials of CPR intervention. Van Horne told a *Globe* reporter, "We were somewhat in the position of a girl who had once been whoring, but who had reformed and was trying to lead a correct life — it was difficult to make everybody believe it." As it turned out, the railway's reform was not complete: in Winnipeg, CPR personnel actively supported the Conservative candidate.

Although he was not directly involved in the 1896 election, Van Horne was still vitally interested in the outcome and what it would mean for several issues that were important to him. Immigration was one of them. He dismissed the Conservative government's work in this area as "hardly visible" and, as seen in chapter 6, he devised an ambitious settlement scheme of his own. Regrettably, the government never adopted it. He expected the new Liberal government led by Wilfrid Laurier to give immigration the same short shrift, but the dynamic Clifford Sifton, the new minister in charge of immigration, worked tirelessly to revamp the lacklustre immigration service he had inherited and to fill the empty prairies with suitable agriculturalists.

As much as he respected Sifton, however, Van Horne took strong exception to his choice of immigrants, many of whom came from eastern and central Europe. In typically blunt fashion, Van Horne outlined his concerns to newspaper editors. One of these was Sir John Willison, the long-time editor of the *Globe*. Van Horne bombarded him with letters about the growing anti-Chinese agitation sweeping the Pacific coast which, he feared, would culminate in increasingly restrictive legislation against Chinese immigration. Like other Canadian industrialists, he wanted access to a plentiful supply of cheap, hardworking labour, and the Chinese filled the bill admirably. "We must have in British Columbia a good supply of digging machines which, unlike steam shovels, can climb hills and go down into mines. These can be most cheaply and readily had from China," he informed Willison.

From time to time in these years, Van Horne was asked to serve in a semi-diplomatic role because of his friendship with leading American political figures. He became a quasi-ambassador to Washington for the new Laurier government, which frequently asked him to probe the Yankee frame of mind during a period of tension between Canada and the United States. Tariffs and the dispute over the Bering Sea near Alaska ranked high on the list of irritants poisoning the relationship between the two countries. It was the tariff question, however, that directly involved Van Horne in his new role. After introducing the two-tiered Fielding tariff in 1897, the government asked him to find out whether the American government would institute reprisals or admit Canadian goods at a rate equivalent to the minimum Canadian tariff. His mission completed, Van Horne informed Ottawa that the United States would certainly not accept any reciprocity proposals.

Van Horne's services were also enlisted in the potentially dangerous Alaska boundary dispute, a dispute between Canada and the United States over the boundary of the Alaskan panhandle running south off British Columbia's coast. The dispute smouldered for decades before coming to a head in 1897, when the Klondike Gold Rush was under way and both the Canadians and the Americans sought control of the trade it produced. After the storm signals went up, Van Horne made another trip to Washington and, in his report, alerted the government to potentially dangerous conditions in the Klondike mining community. In a letter to the leader of the Opposition, he warned that even a trivial ill-advised move by Ottawa could trigger another Boston Tea Party, only this time in the Yukon.

In the 1890s, discerning friends and colleagues realized that Van Horne's enthusiasm for his job was waning. His loss of interest was due to several setbacks, such as his failure to establish a fast Atlantic steamship service — a fallout from the financial panic of 1893 — and the mortifying surrender of the Duluth and Winnipeg Railroad to James Hill. There was also his deteriorating health, brought on by years of overwork, smoking, and self-indulgence in food. More than anything else, though, it was probably the lack of scope for his creativity that robbed Van Horne of his enthusiasm for the presidency. He was essentially a "constructor," a man who loved building for its own sake. Once the CPR was nearing completion, he began to lose interest in it and to find management details more and more distasteful.

In the final years of his presidency, Van Horne talked increasingly of retiring, only to be thwarted by Shaughnessy, who was "anxious to see our affairs in fairly good shape during his Presidency." By 1899, when the CPR was paying substantial dividends, Van Horne believed that condition had been met. Before resigning, however, he decided to take an extended vacation trip. Japan was one possible destination. He had many friends there and the inauguration of the Pacific steamship service had earned him the gratitude of the emperor and government officials alike in Japan. Van Horne, however, had qualms about being on the receiving end of lavish attention and hospitality. He disliked ostentation of any kind and cringed at the thought of the ceremonial observances that would mark a visit to that country. He therefore decided to postpone a trip to that far-distant land and to travel instead to southern California, hoping that the heat there would "burn out" his chronic bronchitis.

With a party of friends, he set off in the *Saskatchewan*, his private rail car, in April 1899 for San Francisco. There, John Mackay, the Dublin-born head of the Commercial Cable Company, booked the best rooms for them in the luxurious Palace Hotel, stocked them with the finest cigars, and refused to allow anybody to pay for anything. After a week of festivities in the city, Van Horne's friends returned to the East, and Van Horne, along with Mackay and the manager of the Southern Pacific Railroad, took the train to Monterey, stopping first at Palo Alto. While in Monterey, Van Horne decided he had been away long enough. He immediately telephoned for his car to be hitched to the next train and, in a few days, he was back in Montreal.

After he had returned home, Van Horne took the bold step he had been contemplating for months: he resigned from the CPR presidency. Many outside observers had been expecting it for some time. Their suspicions had earlier been confirmed when a newspaper reporter, acting in response to rumours, had inveigled an admission from Van Horne that he intended to resign. No date had been provided, but the published account of the interview precipitated a selloff of Canadian Pacific stock. In both London and New York, the price of the company's shares dropped several points. Confidence in the CPR was only restored when its officers issued a denial of the newspaper story. On June 12, however, Van Horne presented his formal resignation at the company's regular board meeting. The directors chose Thomas Shaughnessy to replace him, but Van Horne was kept on as a director and was immediately appointed to the newly created office of board chairman. As chairman, he was an *ex officio* member of the CPR executive committee, so he continued to play a significant role in deciding company policy.

Van Horne could regard the legacy he had turned over to Shaughnessy with justifiable pride and satisfaction. In spite of the prolonged depression that had gripped Canada during most of his term as president, he had managed to improve and expand the system significantly. In fact, by the end of 1899, the extent of the railway's lines totalled seven thousand miles. If the American lines the company owned were included, the increase in the eleven years of his presidency after 1888 exceeded thirty-five hundred miles, or 65 percent. Despite competing interests and his deteriorating health, Van Horne had succeeded admirably in making the CPR a powerful force in the Canadian economy.

8

The Family at Home

Over the years, Van Horne and his family had moved often, following the rapid progress of his railway career in the American Midwest. It must have been a relief when, in 1883, he seemed settled with the Canadian Pacific Railway and the family finally joined him in Montreal.

The stage for this move was set in the autumn of 1882. That fall, the steadily escalating pressure of railway business weighed heavily on Van Horne, both in his office in Winnipeg and in Montreal, the location of the CPR headquarters. It was particularly heavy during his visits to Montreal, when his schedule was chockablock with consultations and interviews. Whether he was in the office or at his hotel, there was always somebody waiting to see him. He put in exceedingly long days and rarely got to bed before midnight. As the construction of the railway forged ahead across the prairies and through the most challenging sections

— the Rockies and the north shore of Lake Superior — the CPR management decided that Van Horne should transfer his own headquarters from Winnipeg to Montreal as soon as possible. Consequently, in November 1882, he took up residence in the venerable Windsor Hotel in downtown Montreal.

At winter's end, in April 1883, the family left Milwaukee and joined him in Montreal. Little Addie was delighted to have her father close by again. During the long absence she had written him often, but always with regret: "The weather is very pleasant and all the roses are in bloom," she wrote in one of her letters. "Those red roses you planted when you came here are one mass of bloom and are the admiration of everyone.... Papa, I wish you would come home, just think! It has been almost 4 months since you was [here] last, we all long to see your dear face again."

Once again, Van Horne had found a suitable home for the family. Like most prosperous businessmen at the time, he chose to live in "the Square Mile," an area on the southern flank of Mount Royal near McGill University where many prosperous English-speaking residents built stately mansions in the last half of the nineteenth century and the opening years of the twentieth. He bought the eastern wing of an imposing semi-detached stone residence that later became known as the Shaughnessy House — after Thomas Shaughnessy, who, in late 1882, was the CPR's purchasing agent. Located at the western end of Dorchester Street, it had been built by CPR director Duncan McInyre, who still lived in its west wing, and timber merchant Robert Brown, who previously occupied the wing that Van Horne purchased. A century later the Shaughnessy House would be integrated into the Canadian Centre for Architecture, but for Van Horne, the location was ideal: the house was close to Donald Smith's

Courtesy of the Notman Photographic Archives, McCord Museum of Canadian History, Montreal, MPMP-000.2345.4.

The Van Horne mansion on Sherbrooke Street West in Montreal. Derided by critics for resembling an armoury, it was razed in 1973 despite a furious campaign to save it.

ostentatious residence — where the Van Hornes would attend many functions — and it was also within a short distance of the CPR headquarters on Place d'Armes, in the heart of Montreal's financial and commercial district.

At the time of the move, there were seven people in the Van Horne family: William and Addie; their children, Little Addie and Bennie; Addie's mother, Mrs. Hurd; and William's mother and his sister Mary. Mrs. Van Horne senior died in 1885, but the rest of them lived in the Shaughnessy House until April 1892, when they moved to a much larger residence at the foot of Mount Royal. It was a neo-classical stone mansion located on the northeast corner of Sherbrooke and Stanley streets. The house, which was probably built in the 1860s, originally belonged to John Hamilton, a senator and president of the Merchants Bank, who occupied it from 1869 to 1890. Critics said it resembled an armoury, but it suited Van Horne. He wanted a bigger house in which to display his ever-growing collections of art and pottery.

Van Horne purchased the property in 1890 and immediately set about to alter it so it would provide the additional space he required. To carry out the remodelling, he hired someone whose work he knew and liked. Edward Colonna was best known as a pioneer of art nouveau, the decorative movement featuring long, sinuous curves of vegetal-inspired forms that was regarded in Europe at the time as the "Modern Style." In the United States, Colonna had worked for Bruce Price, who found a position for him as chief designer for the renowned railway-car builder Barney & Smith Manufacturing Company of Dayton, Ohio. It was there that Colonna probably had his first dealings with Van Horne, who involved himself in the purchase of passenger cars for the CPR. Following his stint with this firm, Colonna stopped off briefly in New York City before heading in 1889 to Montreal. There he opened his own office and renewed his contact with Van Horne, who frequently invited Colonna and his wife, Louise, to meals at the family home. Colonna designed a large portion of the renovation of the Van Horne residence at 917 (later 1139) Sherbrooke Street. In so doing, he provided Canada with a unique example of art-nouveau decoration, and Van Horne with a ground-floor interior that reflected his essentially "modern" taste.

Montreal, with a population of approximately two hundred and sixty thousand, was by far Canada's largest city. In terms of financial clout and entrepreneurial spirit, it was the capital of Victorian Canada as well. A century earlier the North West Company had brought wealth and power to the city from the West. Now the Canadian Pacific Railway would do likewise. But this would occur only after the long depression (1873–96) ended and prosperity returned to the United States and Canada. When that happened, in 1897, the city and the province embarked on a period of renewed prosperity and rapid industrialization.

Montreal's commercial aristocracy controlled not only the province of Quebec but also two-thirds of Canada's wealth and the majority of the country's major corporations. Most of these businessmen lived in the Square Mile, which was then at the peak of its influence. This powerful Anglophone community was British to the core. In slavish imitation of London society, the Square Mile denizens rode to hounds, imported servants from Britain, copied British social mores, and occupied mansions that were surrounded by acres of lawn, orchards, and gardens. Although Sir John A. Macdonald's National Policy and the building of railways by the Grand Trunk, the Intercolonial, and the Canadian Pacific had helped to create this moneyed class, almost all its members had not been raised in privileged circumstances. The CPR duo Donald Smith and George Stephen were typical: both were from humble origins. Smith was the fourth child of a hard-drinking saddler, and Stephen, his cousin, was the first child of a carpenter who had a large family to support. (Stephen became Lord Mount Stephen in 1897.) Robert Mackay, another Square Mile resident and Van Horne friend, was the son of a crofter. Smith, Stephen, and Mackay were all Scottish born, but even those members of the Square Mile aristocracy not born in Scotland were Scottish to "the marrow of their souls." No matter what their religion or background, "they knew how to parlay endurance of the spirit into earthly salvation," according to Canadian journalist and author Peter C. Newman.

Certainly Van Horne knew how to make the most of his time here on Earth. Nevertheless, the fearless optimism that governed most of his life and his extravagant displays of affection for his family ruled out any claim to his being Scottish. So did his gambling instincts, his delight in high living, and his love of big practical jokes. Like most Victorian men, Van Horne was the authority figure in his family. He controlled the family purse and made all the important decisions, although he did consult Addie from time to time. Unlike many other men in his circle, however, Van Horne doted on his wife and children. The role of remote husband and father was not for him. Perhaps because of his own father's early death and the straitened circumstances in which he left the young family, Van Horne craved a sense of security. The love of a devoted wife and a closely knit family became all important to him. His extended family and Addie, with her remarkably serene spirit, became indispensable restoratives for his soul, and he worried constantly about their well-being when he was away from them. Still, like many men of his era, when he went to distant places such as Europe or the west coast of the United States, he travelled in the company of other men and left his wife to look after the children and the home.

In letters to his wife, Van Horne frequently chastised her for being a poor correspondent and fretted about her health. "I am much distressed by your letter of yesterday and as I know you have been and are still seriously ill. I trust that you have not failed to call a doctor," he wrote Addie in October 1872, just after he had moved from Chicago to St. Louis. "If you have not done so do it at once. You must take no risks nor trifle with your health," he continued. To drive home the point that his instructions must be obeyed, he added, "I am *very* busy but am so nervous on your account that I can hardly do anything. Do not fail to let me hear from you every day. Now my Treasure, do not forget that I am anxious about you and that I will be in agony if I do not hear from you and if I do not hear that you have called the doctor." Unfortunately, there is no indication in this letter or in any subsequent correspondence of the nature of Addie's illness. Nor are there any hints as to why Addie's health should have been a source of recurring concern to family members. As it happened, although six years older than her husband, she outlived him for a full fourteen years.

Addie was fortunate in having Van Horne's sister Mary as an indispensable helpmate in running the household in Montreal. This was no light task in a day of large families, big houses, and high housekeeping standards. However polished the butler might be, and no matter the efficiency of the housekeeper and her large staff, Addie was expected to take a personal and informed interest in her kitchen, linen room, and garden. Van Horne's sweet-tempered sister not only played a leading role in numerous local organizations but also rendered invaluable assistance to Addie. She helped out with grocery shopping, raising the children, and entertaining the countless guests who passed through the doors of the Sherbrooke Street mansion. Her death in 1904 at the age of only forty-eight left a yawning void in the family.

Van Horne was certainly conscious of the magnitude of his wife's responsibilities, yet he was not inclined to lavish favours on her. His parsimony, in fact, upset young Addie, who, in her last teenage year, pointed out to her adored father that his wife was "the only lady in Montreal of high position who has not her own horses and you know it does not look well for the wife of the President of the C.P.R. to go calling in cabs or what is worse for her on foot."

For her part, Addie was devoted to her demanding, restless husband. A quiet, intelligent woman, whom the Canadian novelist William A. Fraser described as "the most gracious woman I have ever met in my life," she was ideally suited to providing the solace and support that Van Horne desperately needed in his harried professional life. It is a reflection of how highly he regarded her intelligence and judgment that he consulted her about major career decisions. Despite her college education and musical talents, however, Addie was content to remain in her husband's shadow. For her, home was where she belonged, and, if given a choice, she would have shunned the glimmer and glitter of stuffy Montreal society altogether. Outside the home, she contented herself with serving as vice-president of the women's branch of the Antiquarian Society, attending musical recitals of notable artists, and exhibiting regularly at flower shows.

Although satisfied to play the role of the model late-Victorian wife, Addie at times complained about her lot. Similarly, she occasionally resented her husband's directions. Like so many successful men, Van Horne could be opinionated and dogmatic: he always knew what was best. This superiority could, of course, annoy people, particularly when he proved to be wrong. One day after Addie viewed a display of wedding presents received by a Miss Lonsdale, who married her cousin John Lonsdale Gilman in December 1885, she wrote gleefully to Mary, her sister-in-law:

> The presents were many, pretty and useful — I selected a beautiful card receiver — best plate. I showed it to Will who said "No one ever sent plate. I might throw that away." So I changed it for a pie knife solid only a trifle more & not half as pretty. There were ever so many plated silver articles — There was a coffee & tea service from Mr Gilman's mother & a pretty silver five o'clock tea set from Mr and Mrs Finlay. I asked Mrs F if the large service was solid. She replied "She thought not hers was not." So I looked

> closely at the rest & concluded mine was among the few solid pieces. So I quite enjoyed telling Will he was sometimes mistaken.

Addie was often forced by circumstances to be a gracious hostess — a role expected of the wife of a Square Mile resident, especially someone as prominent as her husband. Because Van Horne, like Lord Strathcona, gloried in it, entertaining was elevated to a high art in the Van Horne home. With strangers and mere acquaintances, and in formal social situations, Van Horne could be cold and austere, if not downright shy. With friends, however, he was genial and gracious. As someone who revelled in the role of courtly host and paterfamilias, he orchestrated countless dinners, Sunday lunches, and overnight visits. While away from home, he would pepper Addie with instructions regarding plans he had for entertaining friends and business associates when he returned. People from all walks of life and occupations figured in his plans: CPR contractors, judges, railway titans, artists, politicians, financiers, industrialists, and writers all enjoyed lavish and warm hospitality at his Sherbrooke Street mansion and at Covenhoven — his beloved New Brunswick estate.

When he was in New Brunswick in the late 1880s to negotiate the lease of the New Brunswick Railway Company to the CPR, Van Horne stopped off in the small resort town of St. Andrews in the southwestern part of the province. He was so struck by the beauty of Passamaquoddy Bay and its islands that he set about acquiring property on Minister's Island, a five-hundred-acre strip of verdant land located a half-mile offshore and around a point from St. Andrews. Over the next couple of decades he put his diverse talents and still formidable energy to work transforming four hundred acres of the island into a self-sustaining estate — not only a large summer home and sprawling gardens but also an impressive working farm and assorted outbuildings. Until the end of his life, Covenhoven would be Sir William's refuge, the haven to which he retreated during the summer and the early autumn in search of rest and creative renewal.

Van Horne acquired his Minister's Island property piecemeal, starting in 1891. That year, he bought one hundred and fifty acres at the most southerly end of the island. Five years later he purchased another two hundred and fifty acres. Addie, after his death, acquired the island's remaining hundred acres in 1926. Once he had purchased his parcels of land, Sir William set out to design a summer home that he named Covenhoven in salute to his father and his Dutch ancestry. The actual construction began in 1898, but unidentified problems soon arose. Forced to seek assistance, Van Horne turned to a young Montreal architect, Edward Maxwell, who, with his younger brother William, would go on to create one of the most significant architectural practices in Canadian history. As soon as Van Horne issued his call for help, Edward hurried to Minister's Island to rectify the construction problems. His intervention succeeded and, when Van Horne decided the following year to enlarge the modest dwelling, he called on Edward once more. The end result was a house that, again, was large and bulky like Van Horne himself. Further additions and modifications were undertaken in subsequent years. All were closely supervised by Van Horne, who sometimes found it necessary to drop everything in Montreal and hurry to Minister's Island to inspect some new construction.

Of all the wings that were added to the main house over the years, the addition that contained his grandson's nursery was probably the one that most involved Van Horne's attention. It was in this room that he lovingly painted a joyous mural for

Courtesy of Library and Archives Canada, PA21681.

A partial view of the family home at Covenhoven, the impressive Van Horne estate on Minister's Island, New Brunswick. Dignitaries from across North America and around the world visited here during the summer months.

small William — Bennie's son. This room also featured at least one mantel constructed of Dutch picture tiles that Van Horne ordered specially from Montreal.

Besides helping to design the original house, Van Horne also turned his attention to planning the farm manager's house, one of several buildings on the large working farm that he envisaged for Minister's Island. Without question, the most impressive farm building on the property was the massive barn, which became the centrepiece of the entire operation. Three storeys in height and built on a stone foundation, it had twenty-five windows on the ground floor alone and boasted a kitchen equipped with an elevator that provided access to the upper floors. Two immaculately kept floors housed Van Horne's prized herd of Dutch belted cattle, so called because of the large white band this breed displays over the shoulders. To Van Horne's delight, these cattle went on to win many show ribbons, including some from the prestigious Royal Winter Fair in Toronto.

Determined to make Minister's Island as self-sufficient as possible, Van Horne installed a fresh-water system on the property: a windmill, assisted by kerosene-fired engines, pumped water from an artesian well to the main house through a system of hydrants. He arranged for a supply of gas for lighting and cooking: in an adjoining plant, when carbide pellets were dropped into water, the resulting gas was collected and piped into the family home. He also grew a vegetable garden and raised sheep, cattle, pigs, turkeys, and guinea fowl. In his own inventive way, he was the best of pioneers.

Even when not at Covenhoven, Van Horne immersed himself in myriad details relating to the estate's operation. His manager consulted him on a wide range of matters, from the castration of a bull to the grading of turnips for sale. In addition to the property manager, the outdoor staff included a head gardener, four assistant gardeners, an assistant stockman, three teamsters, a weir manager, a farm hand, a head field hand, poultry hands, carpenters, plumbers, and painters. Over them all, Van Horne reigned as the ultimate decision maker.

Van Horne always claimed that one of Minister Island's attractions was its relative inaccessibility from the New Brunswick mainland. Still, he could not be long without the company of stimulating friends, and he loved to show people around his estate. They included leading Canadian and American businessmen, railway barons, Japanese royalty, retired generals, and capable women such as Maud Edgar, the principal of a Montreal girls' school. Invitations were also extended to lesser mortals too, and Van Horne, the consummate host and teacher, made everyone feel quite special. Visitors arrived by train or yacht on the New Brunswick coast and usually crossed to the island at low tide on the natural gravel bar that links it to the mainland. Once there, they journeyed for half a mile through woodland before emerging on the estate's expansive grounds. There, waiting for them at the door to the mansion, was their host, who invariably extended the same welcome: "Gentlemen, you may have champagne or milk — the price is the same for both."

Van Horne was a superb storyteller, although in later years he had a tendency to exaggerate. His newspaper friend, Sir John Willison, described him as a gracious host who talked a lot but was never dull or commonplace: "Decisive in judgment and confident in opinion, his sentences were so picturesque and penetrating that even his rasher statements were seldom challenged." Although Sunday was a favourite time to entertain, especially in Montreal, William and Addie also entertained on weekdays. It was not uncommon for the couple to lunch with friends at their home at 917 Sherbrooke Street and then, later that day, meet the same people elsewhere for dinner. Often they accepted written invitations to a meal at Lord Strathcona's fine house. The wealthy, bearded financier had come a long way since he toiled for three decades as a Hudson's Bay Company trader in Labrador and acquired what Governor General Lord Minto contemptuously referred to as a "squaw wife."

Invariably, the menu was extensive. On Tuesday, January 3, 1893, for example, eighteen people assembled around the Van Horne dining table to consume a dinner of consommé, boiled cod with anchovy sauce, partridge pâté, ox tongue with mushrooms, saddle of mutton, turkey with celery sauce, potatoes, peas, celery root, English pheasant with port-wine sauce, frozen chestnut pudding, celery and cheese, Neapolitan ice cream, pineapple water-ice fruit, coffee, and tea. Meals of this nature, not to mention Van Horne's unrestrained appetite, no doubt accounted for his growing portliness and the onset of type 2 diabetes.

Among the guests entertained by the Van Hornes in Montreal was James J. Hill. When visiting Montreal in June 1906 to attend Bennie's wedding, the railway titan arrived on his two-hundred-and-forty-three-foot yacht. Another notable visitor was Rudyard Kipling, who, in 1907, gave rousing speeches on imperial unity across Canada. To provide for their comfort, Van Horne arranged for the famous English author and poet and his wife, Cattie, to have the use of a special private car for their transcontinental train trip. Other visitors included Pauline Johnson, the celebrated Métis poet and entertainer, the popular literary figure Gilbert Parker (later Sir Gilbert), and the American muck-raking publisher Samuel McLure. Canadian artist Wyatt Eaton stayed at the Van Horne mansion for months on end and painted portraits of both Van Horne and Addie.

Among the several art critics who made their way to the Van Horne home was the prominent American Bernard Berenson and his wife, Mary. After one of their visits to Montreal, Mary unburdened herself in a letter to their friend and patroness Isabella Stewart Gardener, the well-known Boston art collector. It was indeed fortunate, wrote Mary, that Isabella had decided not to accompany them on this trip because all they had found in Montreal was provincialism. It was everywhere, but especially in the homes of the Square Mile millionaires, who built "hideous brownstone houses" and "hung in their multifarious and overheated rooms a vast collection of gilt-framed mediocre pictures." Only time spent with Van Horne would have redeemed their visit, she said, but regrettably they could not see him because he was laid up with "inflammatory rheumatism" — a condition that incapacitated him for months during the winter of 1914–15. The Berensons did, however, meet Bennie Van Horne, now thirty-six years old, whom Mary described as "a powerful and intelligent man."

"Powerful" and "intelligent" are not the usual adjectives applied to Van Horne's only son, who had a good mind, but was spoiled and cynical. Perhaps because he was the only son to survive early childhood, Bennie ("Benj" to his intimate friends) became the victim of his parents' overpowering and ultimately destructive love. From his earliest years, he was the centre of attention, doted on by his mother, who fretted about him constantly, and continually instructed by his father, who expected great things from him. Unfortunately, Van Horne never seemed to learn that he could not micromanage people's lives the way he could a railway. Although Bennie graduated from McGill University with an applied science (engineering) degree and, like his father, was an accomplished artist, he never realized his potential. He was essentially unmotivated, lazy, and spoiled. Except for a brief time when he was gainfully employed on one of his father's projects in Cuba, the Cuba Railroad, he remained at home, a ne'er-do-well, drinking too much, running up bank overdrafts, and gambling.

In 1906, Bennie married Edith Molson, the only daughter and first child of Dr. William Alexander Molson, a member of the large Montreal brewing family, and Esther Shepherd, the daughter of R.W. Shepherd, who owned a steamship line. Van Horne was delighted with this match, which linked the Van Hornes with one of Montreal's most respected, wealthy, and powerful families. Moreover, he was fond of his daughter-in-law. After their honeymoon, however, the couple moved into the Van Horne mansion. Van Horne, it seems, was incapable of weaning Bennie from his close control, and Bennie was unable to steer a course of his own.

The marriage produced one child, William, who became Van Horne's adored grandson. Van Horne liked all children, but the love he lavished on this child was beyond reason — and once again destructive. The boy was only eighteen months old when his grandfather began to mould his tastes. As he later wrote, "I wished him to have artistic tastes, so I carried him around to see the pictures. He noticed things in them from the start. Already he can tell ships and birds and the sea, he calls them by name, pats them." When away from home, Van Horne wrote regularly to William, except on a few occasions when the most urgent business scuttled his good intentions. No matter where he travelled, people always inquired about the grandson. Unfortunately, like Bennie, young William developed into a self-centred, pompous child.

Young Addie, in contrast, had no demons to fight. She was a shy woman who inherited her father's big frame and beautiful blue eyes. And she adored her father — they shared an abiding interest in art and identifying and collecting fungi. When Addie was twenty years old, she accompanied her Aunt Mary on a grand tour of Europe. Writing to her brother from Europe in September 1888, Mary told Van Horne that she had decided that his daughter should extend her planned sojourn in Europe in order to see as much of the continent as possible. Hitherto, she explained, young Addie had led a quiet, retiring life, but after her return from Europe she would "have to go into society, where she will meet people who have had all the advantages that travel can give."

After her mother's death in 1929 and the death of her brother, Bennie, in 1931, Addie stayed on in the family home

Courtesy of the Notman Photographic Archives, McCord Museum of Canadian History, Montreal, 11-172901.

Van Horne with small William, the grandson whom he spoilt shamelessly.

on Sherbrooke Street West and continued to manage the Covenhoven estate, which she had inherited from her father. In addition to supporting various charitable activities, she also maintained her father's renowned art and porcelain collections. Even when her eyesight began to fail, nothing gave her more pleasure than to show appreciative visitors around these collections. She knew the location of every exhibit and, when she was almost blind, she drew on her encyclopedic memory to describe the history and features of individual pieces in loving detail. Young Addie died in 1941, after having been ill for some time. She was seventy-two, the same age as her father at his death.

9

The Artist and Collector

Van Horne had a deep love of beauty and art. As a small child, he had drawn pictures on the whitewashed walls of the family home in Chelsea, Illinois. In later life, whenever time permitted, he got out his brushes and tubes and painted a picture — one of his favourite pursuits. At Covenhoven he built a large, well-lit studio in which he produced realistic, somewhat ethereal landscapes, rich in browns and yellows. Often these canvases were inspired by the woods, fields, and shores all around him on Minister's Island.

A rapid painter, Van Horne would frequently complete his canvases — usually large oils — in a single evening from notes he made earlier in the day. He did not labour over his work or spend much time thinking about it in advance because he believed that great art resulted from feeling, not intellect. As he expressed it, "There is no place for intellect in art. Art is wholly a matter of feeling. As intellect enters art goes out.... All of the great artists who acquired temporary fame but subsequently lost the esteem of the world were intellectual. Many of the great artists have been weak-minded or lunatics, or sodden with drink or debauchery." Commenting on the speed with which his friend painted, Robert Wickenden said, "Sir William wanted to paint by telegraph." English-born Wickenden, besides being an artist himself, was also a printmaker, collector, dealer, historian, poet, and cataloguer. He probably met Van Horne for the first time in Montreal, where the Wickenden family lived briefly after moving there in 1900.

On one occasion some admiring friends were dumbfounded to learn that a large canvas depicting birch trees in their autumn glory had been completed in only eight hours and entirely indoors under artificial light. "Yes, but I know what a birch tree looks like," replied Van Horne in response to their exclamations. "Why should I sit outside in the cold to do it? I know the dip of its branches; I know the curl of its leaves; I know the colour of it where the sun touches it in autumn."

Van Horne signed most of his work with his initials, WCVH. Occasionally he substituted "Enroh Nav." This ruse enabled him to indulge in one of his favourite jokes, passing off one of his paintings as either a masterpiece executed by a prominent artist or a work done by an insignificant one. Robert Paterson, a young Scot and an amateur artist, was probably among only a handful of viewers who was not completely taken in. When he visited Van Horne's Montreal home, he stopped transfixed in front of a canvas signed Enroh Nav.

"Who's this by?" he asked.

"Oh that's by an artist of very little account," his host replied.

"Yes, but it's very clever — it reminds me of the work of L'Hermitte, the French landscape painter, but it's signed Enroh

Nav. Oh, it's your own. By Jove, that's good. I didn't realize you were a painter — this has ability." Van Horne chuckled, looked pleased, and with a "humph" passed on.

In Montreal, Van Horne painted in an immense attic studio lit by arc lights. Sometimes the studio was shared by his friend, the Canadian artist Percy Woodcock. According to Woodcock, Van Horne "painted as birds sing, as naturally and enjoyably. It was a form of relief to his creative faculties that were continually seeking an outlet." When sketching outdoors at St. Andrews, Van Horne was sometimes accompanied by George Innes Sr., the American Romantic artist noted for the poetical, mystical landscapes of his later years. One of his choice subjects was Passamaquoddy Bay bathed in moonlight. Van Horne was inspired by the same scene, and he produced a work he entitled *Moonlight on Passamaquoddy Bay*. Although Van Horne loved to paint landscapes and found inspiration from one end of Canada to the other, the self-taught artist did not restrict himself to this genre. Occasionally he ventured into portraiture, sometimes without having his subject sit for him. He once did a portrait of Cléo de Mérode, the celebrated Parisian opera dancer, from photographs.

Van Horne's work was decidedly uneven in quality. Nevertheless, there is no question that much of it was, in the words of his friend Roger Fry, the distinguished British art critic, "marvellously effective and on the spot." Many decades later, in the 1970s, Halifax restorer and artist Robert Manuge commented that the best of the tycoon's work was superb.

Given his love of art and his instinct for collecting, Van Horne quite naturally set out to build an art collection of his own, a hobby he shared with his rival railway magnate James Jerome Hill. Montreal, as Canada's leading centre of commerce in these years, spawned its share of notable art collectors. In addition to

Van Horne, they included such distinguished Canadians as his CPR colleagues Lord Strathcona and R.B. Angus, CPR construction boss James Ross, Charles Hosmer, president of Canadian Cottons and a Bank of Montreal director, the politician and financier George Drummond, and the financier Edward Black. There is no doubt, however, that Van Horne amassed the most outstanding art collection of his day in Canada.

Goaded by his insatiable curiosity and zeal for acquiring things, Van Horne seized every opportunity to study and purchase art. He built up a comprehensive library on art history, greedily absorbed details about the lives of his favourite artists, and scooped up coveted paintings on his many business trips to the world's art centres. He purchased only works that he truly liked. As he once informed a Montreal friend, "A picture that you do not feel you really want is always an incubus and a source of dissatisfaction."

It is likely that Van Horne began collecting art seriously in the mid-1880s, when he was living in Montreal and receiving a large salary from the CPR. Certainly by 1892 he had acquired enough confidence as a collector to begin cataloguing his most prized paintings in a notebook that is now in the archives of the Montreal Museum of Fine Arts. His collection featured works from the early Dutch, Flemish, and Spanish schools (Velázquez, Frans Hals, Rembrandt). It also boasted canvases by such eminent British painters as Hogarth, Turner, Reynolds, Constable, and Gainsborough. And, contrary to what has often been remarked about it, the collection also included many modern works; in fact, all but two of the forty-nine works listed in the 1892 catalogue were from the nineteenth century.

Van Horne distinguished himself by being not only the foremost Canadian collector of his day but also by being the only

Montreal collector to buy works by post-impressionist artists. Timid Montreal collectors shied away from these paintings, but Van Horne was audacious enough to acquire works by Henri de Toulouse-Lautrec, the French graphic artist and poster designer; Mary Cassatt, America's most famous female painter; and Paul Cézanne, the outstanding French painter.

Interestingly, Van Horne's collection in 1892 contained works by several American artists. One of these was the most original and individualistic of the nineteenth-century Romantic painters, Albert Ryder. Van Horne became one of his most stalwart supporters, buying his work, promoting it to friends, and even entertaining the artist in his Montreal home. Van Horne's patronage was not without its drawbacks, however. In their personal dealings, Ryder had to accept criticism and advice — an inevitable by-product of any relationship with the confident and outspoken Van Horne.

At a time when contemporary Canadian artists were shunned by other collectors, Van Horne was bold enough to invest in their work, including paintings by James Wilson Morrice, now considered one of this country's most important artists of his era. In 1906 Van Horne paid what was then the generous sum of $100 for a study of an ox by Maurice Cullen, a member of the Royal Canadian Academy. After viewing Van Horne's art collection in 1936, Toronto art critic Graham C. McInnes rated it as the finest private collection in Canada. McInnes, who championed the work of the Group of Seven as well as that of newer figurative artists, informed his *Winnipeg Free Press* readers that the Van Horne Collection's "richness and variety almost take away one's breath."

Van Horne maintained extremely close ties with the Canadian art world during the closing years of his CPR career. As an honorary member of the Royal Canadian Academy, he attended its annual meetings and exhibition openings. He became actively involved in the Art Association of Montreal (later the Montreal Museum of Fine Arts), and on December 13, 1901, he was elected its president. Although positively niggardly when it came to making charitable donations, he donated $5,000 in 1910 towards the purchase of land and a building for the Montreal Museum of Fine Arts (R.B Angus, in contrast, gave $20,000, and James Ross, $150,000).

As a financier who was keenly interested in investments that appreciate in value, Van Horne was quick to recognize the valuable role that publicity could play in enhancing the reputation of his collection. He welcomed fellow collectors and scholars from all over the world to his Sherbrooke Street mansion, where he personally escorted them around his paintings. On at least one occasion he gave up the whole day to show off his collection to a complete stranger. He also lent pieces to public galleries and museums, many of whose curators heard about his collection from Bernard Berenson, one of several internationally known art critics and connoisseurs with whom Van Horne had dealings.

After Van Horne's death, his art collection of nearly two hundred and fifty pieces, which had been valued at over $1.2 million in 1914, remained intact in the care of young Addie and Bennie. After Addie's death in 1941 (ten years after her brother's), her one-quarter share of the collection was bequeathed to the Montreal Museum of Fine Arts. The rest remained in the hands of her nephew, William. After William's death in 1946, the heirs of that portion of the estate consigned twenty of the most noteworthy nineteenth-century paintings to auction. As a result, works from the Van Horne art collection became widely dispersed.

Van Horne also collected Japanese pottery and porcelain. Although he had never been to Japan, he abandoned fossil collecting in the 1880s and began instead to put together a fine collection of rare Japanese pottery and porcelain. He began buying Japanese pieces less than three decades after Japan had been forced by U.S. Commodore Perry in 1854 to open its ports to trade and Western influences. Almost immediately, the Western world became fascinated by Japanese culture, and objects from Japan began flowing into the West, attracting attention because of their very different aesthetic.

This fad for all things Japanese may have inspired Van Horne to take up his new hobby, though it is more likely that the CPR's inauguration of a temporary service to the Far East in the late 1880s whetted his interest in Japanese culture, especially its pottery and porcelain. Certainly his collection benefited from the CPR's establishment of a regular passenger steamship service to the Far East in 1891. Thanks to this development, Van Horne became acquainted with many Japanese statesmen and prominent businessmen. Once these men learned of his deep interest in Japanese art and ceramics, they began to inform him when choice pieces came up for sale, and sometimes they presented him with valuable gifts of pottery and porcelain. The collection grew steadily in size and value throughout the 1890s and the opening years of the twentieth century. In Roger Fry's opinion, it became the finest Japanese pottery and porcelain collection outside Japan.

Van Horne always handled his Japanese artifacts with great "loving kindness," and, before displaying them to a visitor, he carefully polished them with a piece of soft silk. He loved to contemplate the form, glaze, and decoration of each specimen, and often stood enraptured for minutes at a stretch before a favourite piece. His knowledge of the subject was so extensive that, even when blindfolded, he could usually identify by sensitive touch alone which specimen had been brought to him.

In due time, Van Horne's collection contained a full representation of Japanese master potters. At that point, he turned his attention to still rarer Chinese and Korean pottery. Among the Chinese pieces was a stunningly beautiful, tall, graceful vase made of mottled glass that had once belonged to the illustrious Parisian dealer Samuel Bing Sr. Bing reported that, during his lifetime, Whistler had journeyed several times from London to Paris just to see it. When Van Horne acquired it, he considered it one of his most prized possessions.

In the decade or so before his death, Sir William also assembled a collection of ship models. It boasted some very important old votive models of European origin, made to implore or express thanksgiving for safe passage across the ocean depths. The presence of these vessels in various rooms and halls throughout his Sherbrooke Street home helped to give it the appearance of a domestic museum.

Today, "Renaissance" is an overworked label when it is used in relation to individuals. However, when the term is applied to Van Horne — as an architect, painter, and collector — it is entirely fitting. It is also appropriate that a man so gifted should find outlets for his prodigious energy and talent in so many different pursuits. While these diversions satisfied his collector's instinct and artistic bent, they also served as an important diversion. They distracted him from the many worries and burdens of his job as CPR president and, later, as head of several quite different businesses — the Cuba Company, the Laurentide Paper Company, the Canadian Salt Company, and the Canadian Sardine Company.

10

Cuba Beckons

Van Horne's trip to the West Coast in the spring of 1899, just before he retired from the railway presidency, reinforced his view that he did not want to devote the remaining years of his life to his many hobbies. So long as he had major responsibilities, first as general manager and then as vice-president and president of the CPR, he found that painting and building up magnificent collections of art, porcelain, and model ships enthralled and delighted him. Once he resigned, however, they failed to kindle the same level of interest for him. He realized that hobbies could not fill his life.

At this point, Van Horne was only fifty-six years old, but he knew that his health had been "in an uncertain state for several years." Nevertheless, there was still too much energy churning in his massive frame to allow him to settle into a life of ease. What he needed was a major challenge, one that would tax his problem-solving abilities to the utmost and give a new edge to his life. Alternatively, he said, he wanted a project that involved "working out schemes." Fortunately, just such a project came his way — building the Cuba Railroad.

When Van Horne agreed in 1881 to mastermind the construction of the CPR, he took on a tremendous gamble. That was nothing, however, compared to the audacity he demonstrated in organizing and completing the construction of a railway in Cuba. A developing nation, Cuba had just emerged from nearly four centuries as a colony of Spain. To obtain its independence, it had engaged in a series of minor rebellions and skirmishes that culminated in the War of Independence from 1895 to 1898. At that juncture, the devastated island was acquired by the United States, the victor in the Spanish-American War, which was fought over the issue of Cuban independence. The last stages of this struggle were so costly that starvation and anarchy were widespread. Visible signs of the war's impact were everywhere, from closed schools and abandoned farms and plantations to a wretched shabbiness and stench in Havana, the national capital. There were also fewer people on Havana's streets: for years Spain had herded the rebels and their allies into disease-ridden concentration camps. As a result, the island's population had plummeted from approximately 1.8 million in 1895 to 1.5 million in 1899. There was an alarming shortage not only of labour but also of horses and oxen — all of which were essential to any large construction project in this pre-mechanized era.

To further complicate the problems of doing business, Cuba operated in a bureaucratic nightmare after Spain's departure. Corrupt courts and a chaotic monetary system were everyday facts of life. Combined with the devastation and disease caused by the war, they presented a daunting challenge to the American military government when it took office in January 1899.

Notwithstanding all these drawbacks, Cuba was a country brimming with investment opportunities. In the aftermath of the war, streetcars, bridges, warehouses, sugar storage facilities, and sugar plantations all needed extensive renovation. In fact, no sooner had the smell of gun smoke vanished from the air and shipping been restored than hordes of entrepreneurs began descending on the island eager to snap up development projects. Among these promoters were Canadians who had carved out a niche for themselves in areas that had become Canadian specialties: insurance, utilities, and transportation. Seeking out new investment opportunities, these men came armed with capital from British, American, and Canadian sources.

Competing with the Canadians were American entrepreneurs. Among them was a young man, Percival Farquhar, who would link up with Van Horne and play a key role in the construction of the Cuba Railroad. Farquhar was a Quaker, a trained engineer and lawyer who, during his years at Yale College, had made friends with several Cubans. After a career as a Wall Street speculator, this suave and good-looking thirty-four-year-old left for Cuba to pursue his capitalist dreams. Ultimately, he would come to represent some of the worst excesses of financial capitalism, such as issuing debt on debt and persuading inexperienced politicians to sell state-owned properties at a fraction of their true value.

After arriving on the island, Farquhar set his sights on a scheme to electrify Havana's streetcars, which were then drawn by emaciated mules and horses. The deplorable state of the city's transportation system also attracted the attention of some of Van Horne's business friends. One of these was General Russell

Alger, who had resigned his position as American secretary of war in 1899. Another was the well-known Cuban diplomat, writer, and orator Gonzalo de Quesada. Van Horne, in fact, would later claim that it was Quesada who first drew his attention to investment opportunities in Cuba. Irrespective of who it was, he suggested that Van Horne develop an electrical transportation system for Cuba's capital.

As they had in the past, the twin themes of transportation and money making had an irresistible appeal for Van Horne. Indeed, he was so excited by the prospect of making huge returns from a scheme to electrify Havana's tramway system that he invited William Mackenzie, a corporate empire builder in Canada, and other associates from similar enterprises to form a syndicate to pursue one of the two transit concessions that were then available. To their chagrin, Van Horne and Mackenzie's group lost the bitterly contested fight waged by several syndicates for both prizes. Nevertheless, Van Horne accepted an invitation to sit on the board of directors of one of them — the Havana Electric Railway. No sooner was he on the board than he learned from a prominent Cuban businessman that the company's construction payment rolls contained the names of many fictitious workers. Van Horne immediately recommended that the matter be investigated. "The method of robbery referred to is not peculiar to Cuba," he informed the company's president. "We have to carefully guard against it even here in honest Canada." Unfortunately, the Havana Electric Railway would soon attract a great deal of hostility on the part of American investors who resented its practice of selling stock to Cubans and Spaniards. As a result, Van Horne tried to hide his connection with the company and even refused the presidency when it was offered to him.

Before long, Van Horne became involved in a far more ambitious Cuban undertaking: the building of a trunk railway that would run along Cuba's spine, linking the seaport of Santiago at the island's east end with Havana at the west end. In doing so, it would reduce the travel time between the two ports from ten days to one. As the only trunk railway serving eastern Cuba, the railway would help to open up the country's rich interior and generate wealth. This largely undeveloped interior contained extensive deposits of copper, iron, and other minerals as well as vast tracts of land suitable for cattle raising, the cultivation of sugar cane and tobacco, and the growing of invaluable groves of cedar, mahogany, and ebony.

It was Farquhar who got Van Horne involved in the railway. He had earlier formed a syndicate to pursue his dream and lined up a group of British investors to finance it. When they backed out, he began searching for another investor to replace them. One of the syndicate members, General Samuel Thomas, an ex-president of several American railways, had previously introduced Van Horne to Farquhar. In the spring of 1899, Farquhar approached Van Horne and asked if he would assume the leadership of the syndicate. He lobbied him vigorously, both when they met in New York and by letter to Montreal. Initially Van Horne resisted becoming involved because of the many problems he foresaw: the possible profit did not justify the risk; construction costs were prohibitive; there was an acute shortage of Cuban labourers; many years of "bushwhacking" would inevitably be involved in such an undertaking; and corruption seemed endemic on the island: "Cuba has a liberal supply of artistic liars," he warned, "and several of them are interested in selling their railways."

Still, Van Horne kept a sufficiently open mind on the subject to ask Farquhar to go to Cuba and explore the situation further.

For months the project languished, only to be revived when the young entrepreneur returned to New York with a favourable report on Cuba's outlook. Convinced that the time was ripe, he urged Van Horne to go to the island and take stock of the situation himself. Van Horne had just been elected to the board of directors of the Havana Street Railway, so he agreed and set out on his first visit to Cuba. It became a decisive fact-finding tour that opened a new and exciting chapter in his life.

Once in Cuba, Van Horne was struck by the poor railway system on the island. To serve a country equal in size to Pennsylvania, there were only eleven hundred miles of track, 90 percent of which radiated out from Havana. Additional track encircled the populous seaport of Santiago, but little more than a hundred miles of railway served the largest and richest provinces in the country — Santa Clara, Camaguey, and Oriente. For the most part, these sugar-rich eastern provinces, representing three-quarters of the island's area, could be reached only by water.

Van Horne recognized that there were many drawbacks to doing business in Cuba, but at the same time he grasped the significance of the island's unlimited resources and the prospects for development. He visualized a thinly populated, underdeveloped island transformed by the construction of a railway that linked Havana with Santiago and the city of Camaguey (then known as Puerto Principe), the largest city in the interior. In pushing the CPR through to completion, he had helped to transform western Canada. Perhaps he could now make things happen in Cuba. He had also fallen in love with the island and its people, and he was now prepared to ignore many of the drawbacks that had earlier discouraged him from embracing the railway scheme. He accepted Farquhar's invitation to head up the syndicate.

The first hurdle he had to overcome was the Foraker Act. Enacted by the U.S. Congress in 1899, it prohibited the granting of franchises or "concessions of any kind whatsoever" to foreigners during the American occupation. As long as the Act was in force, any company that attempted to build a railway in Cuba would not have the power to expropriate lands for rights-of-way or to lay track across navigable waters, public property, or public roads. To further complicate matters, any railway project that Van Horne launched in Cuba would have to proceed without a subsidy or land grant. These obstacles alone should have been enough to discourage him from starting any railway venture in Cuba, but the aggressive Van Horne would never let bureaucratic rules stand between him and his favourite projects.

As soon as he had made up his mind to build the railway, he began to ponder ways to get around the Foraker Act — always with the goal of serving the best interests of the Cubans themselves. He thought perhaps that he could evade the provisions of the Act if individuals or a corporation bought separate parcels of private land and then built the railway along these strips. When he checked with a lawyer friend, he learned that there was nothing in Spanish law (which still operated in Cuba even under the U.S. military government) to prevent such purchases. With this assurance, Van Horne charged full steam ahead.

Van Horne was fortunate in having the support of the second U.S. military governor, General Leonard Wood. An army surgeon who had graduated from Harvard's medical school, Wood believed that a railway was essential to make eastern Cuba accessible to the "civilizing" and "modernizing" influences of economic development and to form close ties to the United

States. He therefore aided and abetted the undertaking after receiving assurances that it would benefit Cuba and not merely enrich a few wealthy individuals. Wood and Van Horne soon developed a close friendship.

In March 1900, Van Horne journeyed to Washington to seek the support of the American government. Luck was with him as President McKinley quickly approved the plans when the scheme was outlined to him. It would have been difficult for him to do otherwise because the construction of the railway promised immediate employment for large numbers of Cubans. And once completed, the line would serve as an indispensable catalyst for the development of Cuban resources.

Less than two months after his departure for Cuba, Van Horne was back in Montreal, working feverishly to set up a new company — the Cuba Company — to build the railway. He decided to approach only very wealthy friends and acquaintances, men who could afford to wait indefinitely for a return on their money and who could produce capital during difficult periods when funds and enthusiasm ran low. To ensure that control remained in such hands, he priced each share of stock at $50,000 and limited each shareholder to eight shares. He also inserted a penalty clause stipulating that shareholders who did not contribute an additional 40 percent of their investment when they were asked to do so would have to sell their shares. Unfortunately, recurring shortages of funds later caused him to regret he had not asked for more start-up capital.

To line up the necessary capital, Van Horne made a pilgrimage to New York, where he found himself "in the position of a small boy with his pockets full of bonbons, and all the shares [he] would not let go willingly were taken away from [him]." It seems that everyone he invited to purchase stock did so immediately. As a result, Van Horne had to ask some of the larger subscribers to drop a few of their shares in order to accommodate the wishes of more recent parties. His appeal was ignored. When he returned to Montreal, he had but a small holding for himself, but had managed to line up probably the most impressive list of subscribers ever associated with any commercial enterprise in the Americas.

One of these subscribers was James Jerome Hill, Van Horne's long-time rival from earlier days in the American Midwest. They remained good friends, however, with genuine respect for each other in all things related to railroading. Another subscriber was Thomas Ryan, the vice-president of the Morton Trust Company, though initially he did not jump at the opportunity to join the roster. In fact, he ridiculed Van Horne's bold gambit, contending that "it was a waste of time for him to turn his back on an Empire and go chasing a Rabbit." Van Horne's legendary energies should, he said, be deployed in a scheme that would produce a real empire for him to rule over. The scheme called for Ryan and some of his associates to obtain control of the CPR and then to invite Van Horne to return to it as president. In this capacity Van Horne would work with Ryan's group to extend the CPR further into the United States and so secure for the railway a virtual monopoly of railway activity in North America.

When Ryan described this scenario, Van Horne was both startled and appalled. Then, regaining his composure, he told Ryan that his proposal made a mockery of everything the CPR stood for and that for him to participate in such a scheme would reek of the most vile treachery. Canadians, he curtly informed the financier, regarded the CPR as the backbone of their country, and they would go to any lengths to prevent it from falling under American control. Under no circumstances would he have anything to do with the proposal. This strong rebuff seems only to have impressed the American promoter more, and he immediately reversed his stand on the Cuba Company. He purchased shares in the newly formed company and supplied it with the important backing of the wealthy Morton Trust.

Although Van Horne located the Cuba Company's head office in New York, he incorporated the company in New Jersey because its laws were well adapted to the multiplicity of purposes he had in mind for his new undertaking. He saw the building and operation of the railway as the first step in his plans for Cuba's overall development. Just as the CPR had spawned a host of subsidiary enterprises, so would the Cuba Company. Should his dream be realized, the holding company would develop not only a pioneering railway but also resource-based industries, ports, hotels, telegraph lines, and town sites.

In assembling the management team for the new company, Van Horne, as president, assigned the second top spot to Percival Farquhar, the man who had conceived the idea of a railway to serve Cuba's interior. His unflagging optimism, drive, creative spark, and presence made him the ideal choice to be Van Horne's second-in-command and field commander. Moreover, his generous and mild temperament, the product of his Quaker upbringing, equipped him well for dealing with proud and sensitive Latin Americans.

Once the Cuba Company was established, Van Horne set off on still another trip to Cuba. In the years to come he would shuttle back and forth to the island two or three times a year. Sometimes he made the trip in the company of family members, such as Bennie, but usually he travelled with business or railway cronies he had persuaded to make the voyage. He also made countless visits each year to New York, where much of the Cuba Company's business was conducted and its annual meetings were held. Most often he stayed at the Manhattan Hotel, where he would make himself accessible in the saloon during the evening to anyone who would drink innumerable tankards of German beer and listen to him talk about Japanese pottery, Dutch art, cattle breeding, bacon curing, Chinese script, the ideal planning of cities, and any other topic that interested him. He also mounted several missions to Washington to consult with Americans prominent in Cuban affairs and to lobby on behalf of his railway.

To make this railway a reality, an existing railway had to be purchased, surveys launched, and land acquired. Construction would come next. Van Horne argued that once the necessary authority was obtained to operate a railway and to cross rivers, roads, and other public property that lay between the Cuba Company's parcels of land, very little would remain to be done. In other words, he hoped — and probably expected — that, as soon as an elected legislature had been established in Cuba to replace the U.S. military government, the railway would be so far advanced that no authority could or would want to kill it.

The Cuba Company's first emissaries to Cuba were engineers and land surveyors who arrived in the spring of 1900. The results of their preliminary surveys inspired an enthusiastic report from the chief engineer, who remarked that the country through which the railway would pass was admirably adapted to agriculture. He cautioned, however, that labour would have to be imported as would most of the railway ties and bridge timber. Moreover, because of the prevalence of tropical diseases, notably malaria, hospitals would have to be maintained for the men. It was also likely that most of the water would have to be hauled or wells dug to supply it to the construction camps.

Within a few weeks, developments were unfolding so rapidly that Van Horne found himself busier than he had been in years. From both Montreal and Covenhoven he dispatched a steady stream of letters relating to his Cuban venture. In one letter to a friend he confessed, "The Cuban matter is the most interesting one that I have ever encountered and I am looking forward to a great deal of pleasure in carrying it through and perhaps profit as well — a few dozen Rembrandts and such things, which I think will quite fill my capacity for enjoyment." As the undertaking gathered momentum, Van Horne resorted to his usual passion for detail. Just about everything came under his scrutiny, from the unexpected to the mundane. When one of the project's engineers was taken fatally ill, he monitored the situation closely, instructing the attending physician to spare no expense and keeping the engineer's wife up to date on all developments. Nothing escaped his attention. The treatment of railway ties, plans for wooden culverts, the disposition and care of three hundred mules — these were just a few of the day-to-day questions that utterly absorbed him.

When he was dealing with the Cubans, however, Van Horne recognized that their culture and way of life were markedly different from those in Canada, and he went to great lengths to assert the gentler, more sensitive side of his nature. Instead of his usual bluntness, he demonstrated a remarkable finesse and subtlety. To have done otherwise might well have imperilled the whole undertaking. Van Horne knew that, without land expropriation powers, he could not construct a railway unless the Cubans gave their blessing to the enterprise and were prepared to sell him land. He therefore became a model of courtesy and diplomacy in his dealings with the Cubans. When doing his rounds on the island, he always took his hat off when he met a Cuban, and when one of them bowed to him, he returned the bow twice. He also urged Cuba Company employees to show the same courtesy and consideration.

Van Horne made it abundantly clear to company officials that they must avoid any involvement with politics. The Cuba Company, he reminded them, was a strictly commercial enterprise. He was determined that it and its offspring, the Cuba Railroad, would adopt the CPR's official policy of non-involvement in politics — one that had been compromised only occasionally. Still, non-involvement with politics did not rule out cultivating good relations with General Wood and his administration.

Although he steered clear of overt politicking, Van Horne nevertheless conducted his own public-relations campaign. Often this took the form of soothing letters to governors of provinces through which the railway would run. To assuage any potential fears about the scheme, the letters outlined the Cuba Company's objectives and noted that its shareholders were both American and Canadian capitalists who had the greatest faith in Cuba's future. Company plans included not only the building of a railway but also the development of timber resources, the promotion of sugar planting and other industries, and the encouragement of desirable immigrants.

In the early fall of 1900, grading and construction of the railway began at both the Santa Clara and the Santiago ends. It proceeded as rapidly as possible, using a labour force of up to six thousand men. For the most part, these men were well paid and assigned fair working hours. In the early months of construction, however, the majority of Cubans were suspicious of the Cuba Company's intentions, regarding it and Van Horne as agents of the U.S. government. Soon, however, Van Horne's method of conducting business in Cuba and the railway's perceived benefits won over increasing numbers of Cubans to his enterprise. By January 1901, the Cuba Company and its railway undertaking had come to be regarded as a benign, if not positive, addition to the island scene. This good fortune was frequently offset, though, by problems in obtaining clear legal title to properties it acquired. Van Horne therefore recommended to General Wood that Cuba implement the Torrens land registration system then in use in Australia and in two western Canadian provinces. Invented by David Torrens, it is a system of land title whereby a state-maintained register of land holdings guarantees an indefeasible title to all the properties registered in it.

The Cuba Railroad in 1910.

Notwithstanding the relative ease with which the Cuba Company had obtained rights-of-way and land for stations, there was growing offshore opposition to Van Horne's railway. This opposition originated principally in Washington, where the Cuba Relations Committee received many complaints about it. Some parties charged the Cuba Company with being a monopoly. Other legislators, who had been harassed by aggressive American promoters seeking railway franchises in Cuba, even tabled anti–Van Horne resolutions in the Senate. Most disquieting was a complaint against Van Horne that a New York lawyer forwarded to both the secretary of state and Senator Foraker accusing Van Horne of "flagrantly violating with audacious subterfuges" the Foraker Act and Cuban rights.

There is certainly no validity to the charge that Van Horne was violating Cuban rights. From the start, he sought to build a railway that would aid Cuba's development without depriving Cubans of their territorial rights and independence. And this he succeeded in doing. But there is also no question that, in constructing a railway on private and federal land, Van Horne resorted to ingenious and audacious means to subvert the intent of the Foraker Act.

What was drastically needed was a clear and simple railway law that embodied the best features of Canadian and American railway laws. Van Horne therefore embarked on a self-appointed mission to convince General Wood of the need to substitute such a law for the Texas Railroad Law that Wood was intending to implement in Cuba — and here he succeeded, too. Accordingly, in the summer of 1900, Van Horne set to work on a railway law designed to govern the organization of Cuban railway companies and the building and operation of their lines. On his frequent visits to New York in these years, he and Farquhar often worked on the law at opposite ends of the large desk they shared in the company office at 80 Broadway.

To lobby for the adoption of this law, Van Horne set off in February 1901 for Washington, where he presented his case to various senators. Unfortunately, all his strenuous lobbying was to no avail. The politicians deeply involved in Cuban affairs were totally preoccupied with the friction that had developed between the American government and the Cuban delegates to the constitutional convention that met at Havana between November 5, 1900, and February 21, 1901.

Underlying the strained relations was a series of American demands on Cuba known collectively as the Platt Amendment. When the amendment was first submitted to the constitutional convention, it was defeated. However, because the U.S. military government would not evacuate from the island unless the amendment was passed, the convention delegates eventually swallowed their nationalist objections and incorporated it in the new constitution. Nine days later the constitution was adopted and, the following May, American troops withdrew from the island. In name, Cuba became an independent nation, though in fact it remained an American protectorate.

Van Horne's railway law therefore did not come into force until February 1902, after it had undergone several revisions. In the final stages, Van Horne rarely saw the light of the Caribbean day as he and a phalanx of lawyers toiled away in Havana, putting the final touches to the legislation. The time was well spent, for the end result was a model law based largely on Canadian railway law. Before the law was implemented, however, Van Horne was forced to take extraordinary measures to overcome a series of obstacles. Fortunately, his inventive mind produced solutions that allowed railway construction to proceed.

In 1902 Van Horne and the Cuba Company faced a host of daunting challenges. Not the least of these was a glaring shortage of funds, triggered by delays in the delivery of rolling stock and soaring construction costs. Both were largely attributable to Van Horne's insistence that railway equipment be the equal of those in general use by the best railways in the United States. Cars equivalent of those in general use in Cuba were not good enough. However, to satisfy such requirements, orders had to be placed with the few American manufacturers that could do the work. The inevitable delays threw many a kink into Van Horne's timetable and produced cash shortages. Indeed, soaring costs swallowed up all the remaining funds for railway construction. In the financial crisis that followed, Van Horne had no choice but to turn to fundraising. He asked twenty-two shareholders to provide additional funding, but not all of them did so. The problem was only temporarily resolved when a British financier came to the rescue. Once the financial squeeze had passed, construction proceeded rapidly, only to be interrupted again by unusually severe spring rains that badly eroded clay embankments and cuttings.

Finally, on November 11, 1902, the task was done. Van Horne made a special visit to Cuba to witness the driving of the last spike on the Cuba Railroad's main line. While there, he took a ride on the railway from Santa Clara to Santiago and then back to Ciego de Avila, where the company's principal construction headquarters were then located. All along the line he was enthusiastically received. When he stopped at Puerto Principe, he was feted at a banquet in his honour. At Ciego de Avila he was greeted by practically the whole town, including seven hundred

Courtesy of Library and Archives Canada, E002107474.

A locomotive employed by the Cuba Railroad.

schoolchildren. Never able to resist an opportunity to be with children, he took time out the next day to visit their large school.

The spate of public appearances and tributes did not stop there. Further recognition came from a local Spanish club, which entertained Van Horne and subsequently made him its first honorary member. The municipality of Puerto Principe (it adopted the native name Camaguey in 1903) also rose to the occasion. Before the year was out, it conferred on Van Horne the title "Adoptive Son of Camaguey" for all that he had done to encourage the city's advancement and prosperity." This honour was well merited because, on the city's outskirts, Van Horne constructed a magnificent villa, San Zenon de Buenos Aires. Nearby he established a large experimental farm, emulating a large stockbreeding farm he had set up in East Selkirk, Manitoba.

The railway that was generating so much attention was now operated by a separate company, the Cuba Railroad Company, which was established in 1902. Despite an encouraging start, however, it faced challenges in raising funds for expansion and for the construction of sugar mills. From the beginning, Van Horne had envisaged the erection of sugar mills as part of his grand scheme for the development of that part of the island. With that in mind, he embarked on an exhaustive study of the sugar industry. But all his elaborately laid plans began to evaporate when the financial recession of 1903 intervened, drying up funds for both mill construction and the building of railway feeder lines. Only when the end of the recession freed up funding was he able to forge ahead with his ambitious program. In addition to mills and feeder lines, this plan included the construction of hotels, the establishment of a steamship service between Santiago de Cuba and Jamaica, the creation of an agricultural department within the Cuba Company, and the cultivation of extensive gardens on the grounds of each railway station. In time, the agricultural department carried out experiments on Cuban fibres and other products, issued bulletins, and corresponded with manufacturers who were potential buyers of these products.

As town sites sprouted alongside the railway's main line, branch lines began to snake out into the undeveloped countryside. Repeated shortfalls of capital, however, played havoc with Van Horne's plans to forge ahead steadily with branch-line construction. The cash shortage can be attributed partly to his lack of foresight, but that is not the entire explanation. In the post-1902 years other factors were also at work. One of these, of course, was the 1903 recession. Another was the insurrection that erupted against President Estrada Palma's administration in 1906. This uprising scared away investors and precipitated a drought of investment capital.

Notwithstanding all the setbacks, by June 30, 1910, the railway boasted eight branches in addition to its main line. Included in thc company's rolling stock were sixty-five passenger cars, but as yet no dining cars. Until these arrived, passengers took their meals at picturesque little restaurants that had been designed under Van Horne's supervision. Not surprisingly, he looked to Cuba's rural architecture for his inspiration for these designs.

Towards the end of his life, Van Horne admitted that Cuba had involved him in far more work and worry than he could have imagined when he began the railway project there. Although the admission was painful, he also confessed that he had yet to reap any return on the large amount of money he had invested there between 1900 and 1909. Nevertheless, he took comfort in the realization that he had been of some use in "helping the people of that lovable island."

As for the Cuba Company's shareholders, they did not reap much in the way of returns before Van Horne's death in 1915. Success would come only after the First World War destroyed the European sugar-beet industry, and the price of Cuban sugar skyrocketed from two cents a pound to twenty-three cents.

11

Chasing the Money

"Mackenzie thinks there are 'millions in it' if we can get it into reasonably secure shape," a jubilant Van Horne wrote to his friend General Russell Alger in 1898. "It has been a long hunt and we mustn't miss it." Although Van Horne was writing about the scheme to electrify Havana's tramway system, he could have been referring to any of the numerous other overseas and Canadian projects he became involved with after he resigned from the CPR.

In these final years of his life, Van Horne dedicated himself to making money and savouring the excitement that comes from discovering new opportunities for doing so. Unlike some financiers, he found no joy in stuffing securities away in a safe. For him, money was a means to an end, a way to renovate houses, perhaps, or purchase works of art. He became involved in a staggering number of companies: by some estimates he was a director of at least forty companies, and he invested in countless more. In addition, he played an active role in the management of several enterprises — of which the Cuba Company was the most conspicuous.

From the early days of his career, Van Horne had been a capitalist who venerated the business corporation — he regarded it as the foundation of modern civilization. He once told Sir John Williston that corporations "have souls — composite souls — larger and purer than any individual soul that ever was or ever will be." He added, "I have sat at the Directors' table in corporations for many years and have yet to hear the first deliberately mean suggestion on the part of a Director on any matter of policy and have yet to see the first case in which, as between two lines of policy, the fair and liberal one was not adopted." Van Horne agreed that corporations should pay "their fair proportion of taxes," but, he argued, they "should be taxed precisely the same as individuals are taxed." He saw no valid reason "for making them pay for the privilege of being a corporation, for that privilege is a public necessity and a public good."

From his early years in the United States, Van Horne was always on the lookout for legitimate ways to make money, and he eagerly seized on investment tips his friends and colleagues provided. These he supplemented with the latest business news he gathered via the telegraph. The returns from his real-estate properties and eventually from his extensive holdings of CPR shares, coupled with his large CPR salary, enabled him to amass a fortune. As a dedicated capitalist, he devoted himself unreservedly to nurturing this fortune and making it grow.

Fortunately for Van Horne, his move to Canada opened up an abundance of investment opportunities, particularly after he left the CPR at the turn of the twentieth century. In these years the

Canadian economy moved out of a depression into a period of unprecedented growth, which lasted, with only two minor interruptions, until 1913. During these buoyant years Canada grew faster than any other nation, the United States included. Practically every Canadian indicator soared upward — population, railway mileage, exports, construction, and number of homesteads.

In investing his money, Van Horne always looked to railways, real estate, and companies with tangible assets or intrinsic value to bring the returns he wanted. His real estate holdings included a building in Vancouver and shares in the Montreal Land and Improvement Company and the Winnipeg-based Norwood Improvement Company. Outside the CPR, however, his railway investing was confined to offshore railways, largely in Central and South America. He also invested in a number of Canadian companies that had a product to sell. He succeeded so well that, before he died, Van Horne was recognized as a multimillionaire and one of the most influential businessmen of his generation.

Van Horne began purchasing stock and dabbling in real estate when he was still a young man making his way up the railway hierarchy in the United States. His participation in the business world took on a new dimension, however, in 1894 and 1895, when he became actively involved in organizing the Canadian Salt Company. In due time, this company would carry on business in Windsor, Detroit, and Sandwich. Although Van Horne was still president of the CPR, it eagerly supported this initiative and set out to secure its own share in the Ontario salt traffic. Van Horne would remain president of Canadian Salt until his death.

In the closing years of the nineteenth century, Van Horne also threw himself into the organization and management of several other companies. One of the most prominent among them was the Laurentide Pulp Company (later Laurentide Pulp and Paper), located in northern Quebec. He was drawn into this venture by General Alger, who had made a fortune in the lumber business before becoming secretary of war in William McKinley's cabinet. Alger wanted a group of Canadians associated with him in the enterprise, so he invited Van Horne to become a company director. Van Horne, in turn, wanted to generate more traffic for the CPR, which had a branch line running northward from Trois-Rivières. He was also more than happy to make additional money for himself.

Before long, Van Horne became Laurentide's president. As such, he took an active interest in the erection of pulp mills and power plants and in the production and sale of the company's product. He sank a lot of his own money into it and persuaded a large number of his friends to become investors. The calamity-prone company suffered one setback after another, but in 1902 Van Horne took steps to reverse its fortunes. He reorganized the company and, using a newly discovered process, focused it on the manufacture of paper. Van Horne also took on the laborious task of trying to raise additional capital and, by 1910, the company's prospects had improved so dramatically that it was paying an impressive annual dividend. Five years later, Laurentide Pulp and Paper was the largest paper-making concern in Canada — and Van Horne was considered the "Dominion's greatest business authority on the pulpwood question."

Reorganizing Laurentide should have been challenging enough, but Van Horne, Alger, and some of the company's other investors established related undertakings in the Maritimes. One of these was the Grand Falls Water Power and Boom Company, located in Grand Falls, New Brunswick. When describing its potential to Alger, an ecstatic Van Horne wrote, "The water power company at Sault Ste. Marie are expending $3,000,000 to get forty thousand of horse power, while we will have at Grand Falls nearly twice the power at a good deal less than one-tenth the cost." Van Horne and his associates planned to erect a paper-making mill whose eventual capacity would make it "by far the largest paper mill in the world." They were frustrated, however, by a series of roadblocks, and as late as the spring of 1915 Van Horne was still chasing money for the project.

Neither of these ventures could be described as highly speculative or unethical. Still, some of the others in which Van Horne became involved were "extra hazardous." They reeked of the shady business practices that dominated North American industry before the stock market crisis of 1929. In this era of unregulated business, capitalist barons frequently watered and manipulated stock, or diverted shareholders' and policy holders' money into extremely speculative undertakings. Van Horne certainly did not instigate such practices and schemes. Next to losing a family member, he dreaded nothing more than having his good name sullied by any hint of scandal. Nevertheless, he did allow his name to be associated with some questionable ventures and companies.

Heading the parade were schemes initiated by his young protégé Percival Farquhar, who constantly sought new ways to make money — organizing a new railway, installing an electrified trolley line, or establishing an electrical power distribution system. An avid risk-taker, he shuttled restlessly around the Atlantic in his quest for new money-making projects. Frequently he found them in undeveloped Latin America, where gullible politicians were hungry for modern development. Whenever his search turned up a promising-looking project, he would assemble a syndicate made of bankers, investment dealers, and well-heeled capitalists to invest in the enterprise.

Invariably, Van Horne was sucked one way or another into Farquhar's schemes, sometimes to his great regret. Such was the case with a railway project in Guatemala. Initially Van Horne spurned the idea of becoming involved, feeling weighed down by his many responsibilities and the steady demands being made on his pocketbook. But then he capitulated, no doubt because of his friendship with Farquhar and his gratitude for his services to the Cuba Company. The difficult terrain across which the new line had to be constructed, coupled with political strife and open warfare, unleashed a host of problems. During Guatemala's war with Honduras, Salvador, and Costa Rica, all outside funding for railway construction was cut off. As a result, syndicate members had to dig into their own pockets to find the necessary finances to complete the line. Van Horne found himself pressed for funds — probably because he had invested more than he had intended to in Cuba — and he was forced to sell some of his investments in Mexico. He even had to sell part of his interest in the Guatemala Railroad to Farquhar and other parties. In short, by his own admission, he "suffered severely" from his involvement in the railway. To assume his share of the financial burden, he made sacrifices in both money and time.

Van Horne's association with the Guatemala Railroad, and then with the Brazil Railway, served only to increase his apprehension about the way Farquhar operated — particularly his lack of attention. Although Farquhar was expected to spend most of his time supervising the Guatemala Railroad's progress, he was, instead, chasing opportunities in Brazil, Colorado, and Alaska. "Success is only possible in taking up one thing and sticking to it exclusively, until it is worked to a conclusion," Van Horne wrote indignantly to his friend. "I regard failure as certain in every one of those enterprises which depend largely on you."

So disturbed was Van Horne about Farquhar's way of operating that he tried to resign from the Brazil Railway Company as soon as possible. However, although he insisted that his name be removed from all the company's publicity material, it continued to appear among the list of directors for several years. Eventually the railway collapsed, confirming his worst suspicions.

Problems of a different sort confronted Van Horne in his association with two enterprises in the Maritimes: the Dominion Coal Company and the Dominion Iron and Steel Company, both of which were initially headed by Van Horne's friend Henry Whitney, a Boston industrialist. In 1901 Whitney and his associates sold majority control of the two operations to a syndicate led by James Ross, a prominent Canadian financier and railway contractor, who in 1903 sold the steel company to another financier, J.H. Plummer. As a director of the two companies, Van Horne became closely involved in a long and bitter contract dispute between them. At issue was a formal contract that the coal company signed in 1899 with the Dominion Iron and Steel Company to furnish high-grade coal. The dispute degenerated into a protracted battle that first played out in Nova Scotia's Supreme Court. There, Van Horne served as a witness for the steel company, having resigned earlier from the coal company's board. Initially he lamented the litigation and tried desperately to avert it, but once involved, he revelled in detecting and defeating his adversary's moves — just as he had years before in his old railway battles. Eventually the case went all the way to the Judicial Committee of the Privy Council in London (then Canada's highest court of appeal), which upheld the Dominion Iron and Steel Company's case.

Van Horne demonstrated his national vision by investing in British Columbia, where he became a late subscriber in the British Columbia Lumber Company. Another B.C. venture in which he took an interest began during one of his annual western inspection trips. When his train was delayed for some hours at Yale, Van Horne and his party tried their hand at panning the river soil for gold. Soon after, they all invested in a hydraulic mining plant, which developed into the Horsefly and Hydraulic mining companies. They struggled along for several years in the province conducting placer mining operations, but eventually the companies were wound up after much more than the original investment had been lost.

The fortunes of another company in which Van Horne had an interest, the New York–based Equitable Life Assurance Society, attracted a lot of adverse attention thanks to the shenanigans of its principals. The unwelcome publicity did not occur, however, until several years after Van Horne joined the company's board, which boasted several leading American financiers he knew well. Confident that the company was in good shape and meeting its obligations, Van Horne attended board meetings only occasionally, and then only in a perfunctory way. Great was his shock, then, when the society, along with the other two big insurance companies, became the subject of screaming newspaper headlines and eventually an investigation by the New York State Legislature. A series of magazine articles had charged the three firms with systematically bribing regulators and politicians and investing policy-holders' money in risky ventures instead of "safe" government bonds. In 1905, the New York state investigative committee began to take evidence about the scandals. When that investigation revealed serious mismanagement and irregularities, a similar body, the Royal Commission on Insurance, was appointed in Canada in 1906.

Van Horne was shocked by the revelations of misconduct on the part of the North American insurance industry. He was so mortified personally that he began to question the propriety of retaining directorships in companies in which he exercised no control. In 1907, therefore, he began to retire as gracefully as he could from many of them. He still retained an interest, however, in many firms. Several of these firms involved transportation in one form or another, notably street railways and traditional railways. Like other railway tycoons of this era, Van Horne invested in electric street railways, which began replacing horse-drawn trams as a mode of public transit in the late 1880s. Among the urban tramway systems in which he invested were the Toronto Railway Company and the Winnipeg Street Railway, whose reorganization was spearheaded by the wily and crafty William Mackenzie, one of Canada's best-known entrepreneurs in the first two decades of the twentieth century and a leader in the reorganization and electrification of street railways. In Saint John, New Brunswick, Van Horne and James Ross, an aggressive utility entrepreneur, purchased the property of the Consolidated Electric Company and became actively involved in the modernization of the street railway there.

Abroad, Van Horne invested heavily in Latin America. There, his many investments included the Demerara Electric Company in Georgetown, British Guiana, and the Mexican Light and Power Company, whose head office moved from Halifax to Montreal. In Brazil — a vast, undeveloped country brimming with promise — Van Horne became associated with various enterprises blazed by the well-known promoter and engineer, Fred Pearson. One of these undertakings was a holding company formed in 1912: Brazilian Traction, Light and Power Company, headed by William Mackenzie as chairman and Fred Pearson as president. They appointed Van Horne as a director on its first board. He took great satisfaction in knowing that the company, Brazil's largest utility company, was making a substantial contribution to the economic development of southeastern Brazil's industrial heartland.

Launching new companies in an era of unregulated and unscrupulous financial systems and scraping funds together to keep some of them going would have been enough to tax the energies of most men of Van Horne's age; however, it wasn't enough for him. In the late 1890s he decided to expand his role as a hobby farmer by starting a stock farm at East Selkirk, Manitoba, the gateway to the Prairies. He began assembling land for the operation in 1898 while he was still president of the CPR. The farm was intended to draw attention to the district's potential and thereby attract settlers — passengers and freight were essential to the railway's success. Because the farm was intended as a showplace, Van Horne arranged for the "cultivation and ornamentation" of the CPR's right-of-way that stretched over the four-mile length of the property. He also hired Edward Maxwell to draw up eye-catching plans and specifications for the farmhouse and its outbuildings.

Regrettably, the Selkirk operation proved to be a steady drain on Van Horne's purse. Nevertheless, he appreciated the additional opportunity it provided for him to breed stock. Determined that he would become a champion exhibitor, the competitive Van Horne set out to obtain the best stock and to beat rival contenders at the game. He succeeded, acquiring a prize herd of shorthorns that took blue ribbons at shows in Winnipeg, Chicago, and elsewhere.

The farm's drain on Van Horne's pocketbook was imitated by another of his ventures — the Canadian Sardine Company, a giant undertaking founded in 1911 to harvest and can the sardines of Passamaquoddy Bay. Van Horne planned to build a cannery and a model residential village at Ross's Point at Chamcook, just outside

St. Andrews. He found skilled workers knowledgeable about the fishery in Norway, but when the twenty-eight young men and one hundred young women arrived at St. Andrews, their promised accommodation was still under construction. Unfortunately, this mishap proved to be but one of many associated with the enterprise, and it finally closed in 1914. Aside from the original stock that Van Horne purchased, he lost about $100,000 in the venture.

Van Horne lost money in many of the projects in which he was involved, all too often because he lacked the time or the skills to carry out some of his schemes effectively. Still, he was certainly a businessman with vision, as his association with the Laurentide Pulp and Paper Company and the East Selkirk ranch both prove. He lacked the business instincts necessary to accumulate a huge fortune, however, because his restlessness and diversity of interests prevented him from focusing his attention on a handful of promising undertakings and fully exploiting their potential. Nevertheless, he undoubtedly made money in such companies as Canadian Salt, Laurentide Pulp and Paper, Royal Trust, and the Equitable Life Assurance Society. Money-making aside, Van Horne was highly respected by his peers and much sought after as a company director. Perhaps that is why, in early 2000, a blue-ribbon panel of judges assembled by the Canadian Business Hall of Fame voted him the most outstanding business leader of the twentieth century.

12

The Twilight Years

In the spring of 1906, Van Horne took Bennie and Lord Elphistone, a Scottish peer and CPR shareholder, to dinner at Henri's, the celebrated restaurant in Paris. When the Van Horne party arrived, the head waiter rushed forward to receive them, and, to Van Horne's embarrassment, the orchestra played the opening bars of "God Save the King." Such was the price the railway magnate occasionally paid for resembling the portly Edward VII.

Although neither a crowned monarch nor a member of the British or the European landed nobility, Van Horne was a leading member of Canada's financial aristocracy and one of this country's most influential men. As a result, he was frequently invited to accept honours. Because of his odd shyness in formal social situations and his dislike of public speaking, he frequently turned down these invitations. Despite his disdain for pomp and ceremony, however, he did agree on occasion to serve on committees that were charged with a variety of public duties.

In the early autumn of 1901, for instance, he helped to arrange the Canadian tour for the Duke and Duchess of Cornwall (the future King George V and Queen Mary). Van Horne played a role in planning the two days of elaborate ceremonies and festivities that took place in the flag-bedecked city of Montreal. The "new imperialism" then in full swing stressed the superiority of the Anglo-Saxon race and Great Britain's civilizing mission in the world, and the reception committee spared no effort to cement still further Montrealers' ties to Great Britain and the empire. On the third morning of the visit, Van Horne rose early and went to Windsor Station to see the duke and duchess board a special train to Ottawa. He took great pleasure and pride in the royal train that the CPR had provided for the royal couple's transcontinental journey. Two of the seven cars that had been specially built for this trip boasted elaborate interiors complete with telephones and electric lights as well as royal crests on the exterior.

Four years later, in the autumn of 1905, Van Horne again helped to arrange a royal visit to Montreal — this time for Prince Louis of Battenberg, the grandfather of the present Duke of Edinburgh, Prince Philip. From Montreal the prince left for Fredericton and St. Andrews, where he stopped off at Minister's Island to enjoy Van Horne's hospitality.

Although he was now in his sixties, Van Horne found himself even busier than he had been as president of the CPR. Now at the height of his career, he was involved in a staggering number of business enterprises — his supervision of the Cuba Company and the construction of the Cuba Railroad; the administration of his estates in New Brunswick, Manitoba, and Cuba; and his participation in various schemes of municipal and national advancement. There were times, even for Van Horne, when the demands made by these various commitments seemed overwhelming, especially when he experienced health problems.

One of the highly touted federal schemes in which Van Horne became involved was a scheme promoted by Canadian farmers and politicians to construct a shipping canal from Montreal to Georgian Bay. This Georgian Bay Canal Project simmered for decades until the Laurier government publicly committed itself in 1904 to provide funds for it. Van Horne initially embraced the project warmly and did whatever he could to make it a reality. When he studied it more closely, however, he began to doubt the feasibility of constructing a canal twenty-eight feet or more in depth and adapting facilities for it at lake ports. As it turned out, the canal was never built and, in 1917, it was voted down by a special Commons Committee on Railways, Canals and Telegraph Lines.

Notwithstanding the enthusiasm with which he embraced new ideas and schemes, age was catching up with Van Horne — and he knew it. In the wake of the Equitable Life Assurance Society fiasco, he began to relinquish numerous company directorships and, by the spring of 1910, he had withdrawn from about thirty boards. The only severance he regretted was his resignation in 1910, at age sixty-seven, from the chairmanship of the Canadian Pacific Railway. When he retired as president of the railway in 1899, the company's stock sold for $110 a share. Now it was fetching $181.50 a share. As an optimist, he had always believed in the CPR's prosperity, even in the depths of the financial panic of 1893–94. At last it seemed that his unwavering faith in its prospects was more than justified.

Friends expected that Van Horne would now devote more of his time to public service. The Laurier government pointed the way in 1903, when it offered him the chairmanship of the National Transportation Commission. The temptation to accept was great, but Van Horne declined the invitation, claiming prior commitments. When Sir Lomer Gouin, the premier of Quebec, asked him to become a member of Montreal's Parks Commission, however, he agreed. The commission, made up of politicians and businessmen, was established in 1910, when a wave of enthusiasm for city planning, garden suburbs, and parks was sweeping across Canada. Van Horne was an ideal choice, given his long-standing interest in the beautification of towns and cities and his passion for designing structures and gardens, and he welcomed the opportunity to serve on it. Regrettably, the commission's work was hampered by a perpetual lack of funding, accentuated by the recession of 1913. As a result, the body in which Van Horne had invested so much hope was unable to discharge its ambitious mandate. Disheartened, his goodwill utterly exhausted, he suggested in April 1914 that it be dissolved.

The whole experience was certainly disillusioning for Van Horne, especially as his sardine fishery enterprise had also recently collapsed. Fortunately, the other public causes with which he was associated progressed more smoothly. They included the Royal Victoria Hospital, which he served as a governor; McGill University, on whose board of governors he sat; and the St. John Ambulance Association, where he was vice-president.

Outside the public sphere, Van Horne was able to assist the daughter of a prominent liberal friend, J.D. Edgar, to realize her dream of establishing a private girls' school in Montreal. Maud Edgar had taught at Havergal Ladies' College in Toronto, where she found a soulmate in the English-born Mary Cramp, who shared her ideals and advanced thinking about teaching. These two friends began to dream of establishing a school grounded in their teaching philosophy, and they set out to find a suitable building. They finally found one on the western edge of Montreal's Square Mile. The building was available, and soon negotiations were under way with Samuel Carsley, the builder's son. Although Edgar and Cramp had the necessary enterprise to found a school, they lacked practical knowledge about the complexities of leases and risk capital. Here Van Horne came to their rescue: he purchased the Carsley property and assumed the lease that Edgar had taken out with Carsley.

Disaster struck in late January 1913, when fire raced through the school, allowing boarders and the two founders to escape with only their night clothes. In the early hours of the morning, Maud Edgar and Mary Cramp made their way to the Van Horne mansion, where they were provided with overnight accommodation and clothes. Van Horne was in Cuba at the time, but when he was notified of the conflagration, he immediately contacted the insurance adjustors. He also got in touch with his favourite architect, Edward Maxwell, and asked him to direct the necessary repairs. Next he instructed Bennie to look after the Carsley property in his absence, keeping in mind that his father was "anxious to help Miss Edgar in any possible way without throwing away money." Van Horne continued to assist the school in its rebuilding program until January 1914.

Still, despite his kindness to many individuals, Van Horne was downright stingy in terms of charitable donations to hospitals, colleges, welfare organizations, and other organizations that serve the community. His will, drawn up in January 1915, made no provision for bequests to non-profit organizations or charities, nor did it provide for friends or family retainers. By contrast, Lord Strathcona's will listed a large number of generous bequests to colleges, college professorships, and hospitals in Canada, the

United States, and the United Kingdom. During his lifetime, Van Horne did make one or two noteworthy donations to public institutions, but, overall, he hated to part with money that he could use to purchase yet another painting or Japanese vase.

In the final decade of his life, Van Horne continued to shuttle constantly between Montreal and New York and Montreal and Havana. Interspersed with these excursions were transatlantic voyages in luxuriously appointed ships. When he made the crossing to England, it was primarily for business, the renewal of old friendships, and for viewing paintings and other art objects.

In the summer of 1912, Van Horne, accompanied by Addie and young Addie, journeyed to Joliet to participate in the homecoming festival timed to coincide with the July 4 festivities. It had been forty-eight years since he left the town, where he had spent a good part of his youth and where, in his last job, he had been the ticket agent and telegraph operator for the Chicago and Alton Railroad. Now he was the centre of attraction at a public meeting in the town's library — and there he regaled his audience with recollections of his first visit to Joliet as a boy. What most impressed those who had known him half a century earlier was his total lack of pretension. He was still the same Will Van Horne they recalled from earlier days, a man of rough-and-ready comradeship.

The Joliet reunion was so exhilarating that Van Horne returned to Montreal feeling energetic and rejuvenated. He turned his attention with renewed vigour to the construction of his Cuban home, San Zenon de Buenos Aires. Once it was completed, he planned to make it his retreat during Montreal's long, harsh winters.

Van Horne also continued to take a lively interest in the fate of the CPR. Any perceived danger to the company immediately roused him to action, as did any implied threat to Canadian manufacturers or to Canada's ties with Britain. When reciprocity — free trade with the United States — resurfaced during the 1911 election, Van Horne marshalled all his forces to fight it. Canadians were bitterly divided over the issue: the farmers demanded a broad free-trade agreement to eliminate duties on a wide range of natural products and to lower them on some fully manufactured and semi-finished articles; they were opposed by manufacturers and other ardent supporters of the National Policy, who considered tariffs essential in order to nurture Canada's infant industries. Van Horne loudly supported the protectionist side: as he told one reporter, "I am out to do all I can to bust the damn thing." That included addressing public meetings in Montreal, St. Andrews, and Saint John and striving to convert friends and acquaintances to his anti-reciprocity position. In addition, he feared that free trade with the United States "would loosen the bonds which bind Canada to the Empire and ultimately destroy them." When the Liberal prime minister, Sir Wilfrid Laurier, lost the election, Van Horne was ecstatic. He declared: "Canada's first great trial is ended and she now stands out in brilliant sunshine without a cloud in the skies."

Van Horne was quick to offer the new Conservative prime minister, Robert Borden, advice on how best to run his government and even the men he should appoint to certain powerful positions in the Cabinet. Borden ignored his ideas, however, along with his suggestion that the money-losing Intercolonial Railway be administered by three competent commissioners along strictly business lines. Van Horne had stature as a pre-eminent businessman and railway manager, but he could be politically naïve with regard to making Cabinets and fulfilling election promises.

Despite rebuffs, however, he continued his efforts to influence Borden's thinking on various issues of the day.

No social democrat, Van Horne believed that just about anything could be accomplished through effort, determination, and goodwill. To one interviewer he observed that able men have always "appropriated a large amount" of the world's goods and that to deny them these just rewards "would be to send us back to chaos." As a devout family man, however, he was prepared to lobby for legislation that would, he thought, help to preserve the family — the basic unit of Canadian society. Discipline, along with industry, undivided attention to duty, and unswerving loyalty to family, friends, and the CPR, were the tenets that governed Van Horne's life. He attached the greatest importance to discipline, for, to him, it was the foundation of character. It had made possible his climb to lofty heights. He also believed, though, that to reach such heights, men had to be masters of humbug — and among such masters he included his friend and railroading rival James Jerome Hill.

While engaged in a stunning array of activities, Van Horne had to cope with recurring health setbacks and the nagging realization that his overall heath was not good. There had been attacks of bronchitis, but potentially much more serious was the onset of diabetes and a kidney disease, glomerulonephritis, which Van Horne always referred to by its more common name, "Bright's disease." Especially irksome was a lengthy bout of "inflammatory rheumatism" that confined him to bed and home for weeks on end in the winter of 1913–14. Unfortunately, as soon as the rheumatism abated, a carbuncle developed on one of his knees and confined him once again to his bedroom. Never a submissive patient, he openly defied his physician's order not to smoke more than three cigars a day.

When he was finally able to resume his normal life, Van Horne headed directly for Cuba. There, the island's sun and his focus on beautifying San Zenon des Buenos Aires hastened his recovery. In early June, four days after his return to Montreal, he headed for Europe. Accompanied by Bennie, he made what would prove to be his last visit to London. Although business matters absorbed much of his attention, he also sandwiched in a meeting with his old colleague Lord Mount Stephen, an interview with the art dealer Stephan Bourgeois, and a visit to the theatre to see a play selected by Bennie.

No sooner had they returned to Montreal than the First World War broke out. The pugnacious Van Horne had always thought that wars were inevitable and, indeed, a good thing. In 1910, as tensions rose in Europe, his friend Samuel McClure, the American publisher, had raised the topic of war in a letter. In reply, Van Horne stated that he had no use for universal peace and nothing but praise for war as a promoter of man's highest qualities. If worldwide peace reigned, he continued, "I feel sure that it would result in universal rottenness.... All the manliness of the civilized world is due to wars.... All the enterprise of the world has grown out of the aggressive, adventurous and warlike spirit engendered by centuries of war." In 1914, however, he was certain there would not be any war. He had high regard for Kaiser William II and considered him the greatest emperor of all time — he particularly admired his business acumen and economic skills. Van Horne predicted, therefore, that there would be no war with Germany: "The great wars of the future will be in trade and commerce," he declared. He was appalled when the assassination of Archduke Franz Ferdinand of Austria gave way to ultimatums, mobilizations, and declarations of war by major world powers. The aging mogul soon changed his attitude towards war, however, when he realized how awful was its destruction and how tragic was its annihilation of a generation of promising young men.

To escape from the shadow of war and Montreal's harsh winter, he hurried off to Cuba in December 1914. The following year, he made two more visits, one in February and one in May. He also took his grandson, William, on a tour to New York. Other than these trips, he busied himself in Montreal, all the while regretting that he could not play an active role in the war effort. He did, however, put his fertile mind to work creating a detection device that would enhance the Allies' ability to hunt German submarines. He forwarded his suggestion to the British Admiralty, which considered his proposal but then turned it down.

Fortunately, another avenue of service opened up to Van Horne — Prime Minister Robert Borden asked him to chair a federal commission that would examine agriculture, immigration, transportation, the borrowing of capital, and the marketing of food products. Van Horne accepted the invitation, but then hesitated, concerned that his deteriorating health would not allow him to take on two years of almost continuous work. But no other nationally known figure had more qualifications for the job or a deeper interest in the topics to be covered. Borden knew that Van Horne's name would lend influence to the commission's work and credibility to its report, and he responded that arrangements could be made to accommodate Van Horne's absences during the winter months in Cuba. On July 9, 1915, Van Horne cabled the prime minister that he was willing "to take chances" if Borden thought that best.

Shortly after his return from Cuba in early June, however, Van Horne came down with a fever that baffled his physicians and forced periods of rest on him. When his activities were not sharply curtailed by the fever, he made several visits to Covenhoven and continued to manage his various business enterprises. Then, on the night of August 22, he was rushed to the Royal Victoria Hospital, where early the next morning he was operated on for a huge abdominal abscess. To the great relief of the family and anxious friends, the operation was judged a success. Once he rallied from the shock of the operation, he began receiving visitors, some of whom he entertained with plans for the new type of hospital he would build when he regained his health. On September 7, however, he took a turn for the worse and, four days later, he died. He was seventy-two years old.

Messages of sympathy poured in from around the world, while across the far-flung CPR system, from Montreal to London and Hong Kong, flags on company buildings drooped at half-mast. Across Cuba, church bells tolled for the passing of the man who, "in little more than one year had done greater work in Cuba than the Spanish government had accomplished in four hundred and fifty years."

The funeral took place on the morning of Tuesday, September 14, from Van Horne's Sherbrooke Street home, where the service was conducted in the great drawing room by the minister of the Church of the Messiah — the church Addie and his sister Mary attended. The funeral procession then set out for Windsor Station by way of Stanley Street, which was thronged with onlookers. Flower-laden carriages headed the procession, testimony to Van Horne's great love of flowers, particularly lilies and roses. At the station, the coffin was transferred to a special train whose locomotive was draped in black crepe. The train then departed for Joliet, where Van Horne was to be buried in Oakwood cemetery, the place where other members of his family had been buried. The last car on the train was the official car, the *Saskatchewan*, which he had used since 1884. As the funeral train made its way across Canada, groups of men who revered Van Horne's memory greeted it at station after station. In homage to him, all traffic on the CPR system was suspended at an appointed hour.

A year after Van Horne's death, George Tate Blackstock of Toronto, his legal counsel during the frenetic years 1885 to 1892, wrote a fitting epitaph for his friend: "Canadians even today have no realization of the work he did or of what they owe him. He was a Napoleonic master of men, and the fertility of his genius and his resource were boundless, as were the skill and force with which he brought his conceptions to realities."

Chronology of William C. Van Horne

Van Horne and His Times

1843
William Van Horne is born on February 3, 1843, to Cornelius Van Horne, a lawyer, and his wife Mary Van Horne, née Mary Minier Richards. William, the first child of Cornelius's second marriage, is born near Frankfort, Illinois.

Canada and the World

1843
Congress appropriates $30,000 for the construction of an experimental thirty-six-mile telegraph line between Washington, D.C., and Baltimore, Maryland.

1845
A serious blight wipes out about three-quarters of Ireland's potato crop. It returns the following year, causing still more suffering in what becomes known as the Irish Famine.

1846–48
The Mexican War of 1846–48 between the United States and Mexico results in the Treaty of Guadeloupe Hidalgo whereby Mexico renounces claims to Texas and cedes New Mexico and California to the United States.

Van Horne and His Times

Canada and the World

1848
There are revolutions in many European countries, sparked by the February Revolution in Paris.

1851
Cornelius moves the family to Joliet, Illinois, where he resumes his law practice and becomes the town's mayor.

1854
Cornelius dies of cholera, leaving his wife and five children. To help support the family, young William delivers telegraphs from Joliet's telegraph operators.

1855
A railway opens from Halifax to Truro and Windsor, Nova Scotia.

1856
Van Horne, aged thirteen, leaves school and begins to study telegraphy seriously.

1856
The Grand Trunk Railway is completed from St. Mary's to Sarnia, Ontario.

1857
Van Horne, at age fourteen, obtains employment as a telegraph operator with the celebrated Illinois Central Railroad in Chicago. In the autumn of that year, he begins working as a messenger and freight checker on the Cut Off, a forty-five-mile-long line operated by the Michigan Central Railroad.

Van Horne and His Times

Canada and the World

1861
In the spring of 1861, the American Civil War erupts. Before it is over, it will claim over six hundred thousand lives and maim thousands of other participants in body or mind.

1862
Van Horne accepts an offer from the Chicago and Alton Railroad to become its telegraph operator and ticket agent at Joliet.

1864
In 1864, Van Horne is promoted to train dispatcher at Bloomington, Illinois, a Chicago and Alton divisional point.

1867
On March 26, 1867, Van Horne marries Adaline (Addie) Hurd, daughter of the late Erastus Hurd, a civil engineer, in Joliet. After the marriage, Addie's mother Anna and Van Horne's mother Mary and his sister Mary move into a rented house in Bloomington with the newly married couple.

1867
Confederation unites Ontario, Quebec, New Brunswick, and Nova Scotia. Sir John A. Macdonald becomes Canada's first prime minister.

1868
On May 1, 1868, Van Horne is promoted head of the Chicago and Alton's entire telegraph system.

Adaline (Little Addie) is born.

Van Horne and His Times

1869
Van Horne moves his entire family to Alton, Illinois, where he becomes superintendent of the Chicago and Alton's new southern division.

1870
The Chicago and Alton promotes Van Horne to its headquarters in Chicago. There, he becomes assistant superintendent in charge of the movement of freight and passengers over the entire Chicago and Alton system.

1871
William Van Horne Jr. is born on October 8, the same day that the Great Chicago Fire breaks out.

1872
On July15, 1872, Van Horne is appointed superintendent of the St. Louis, Kansas City & Northern Railroad, a subsidiary of the Chicago and Alton. St. Louis, Missouri, becomes the family's new home.

1874
Van Horne becomes general manager of the Southern

Canada and the World

1870
France is defeated in the Franco-Prussian War of 1870. By the terms of the peace treaty she is forced to surrender the province of Alsace and most of Lorraine to the Germans.

1871
Sir Sandford Fleming becomes engineer of the proposed Canadian Pacific Railway. British Columbia joins Confederation.

1873
The Pacific Scandal brings about the defeat of Sir John A. Macdonald and his Conservative government.

Van Horne and His Times	*Canada and the World*
Minnesota Railroad on October 1, 1874. The family moves to La Crosse, Wisconsin. Four years later, he takes on the additional office of president.	
1876 Willie dies of unknown causes on May 17.	
1877 Richard Benedict (Bennie) Van Horne is born in May.	
1878 In October of this year, Van Horne becomes general superintendent of the Chicago and Alton while remaining president of the Southern Minnesota. The family, with the exception of his sister Mary, who remains in La Crosse, moves to Chicago.	
1879 Van Horne accepts an offer to become general superintendent of the Chicago, Milwaukee & St. Paul Railroad. The family moves to Milwaukee, Wisconsin.	
1881 In the early autumn of 1881, Van Horne is invited to become general manager of the infant and faltering Canadian Pacific Railway. He makes a	

Van Horne and His Times	*Canada and the World*
reconnaissance trip north of the border, and after returning home accepts the CPR's offer.	
1882 On January 2, Van Horne takes up his new job as general manager of the CPR.	
1884 Van Horne is made vice-president of the CPR and is elected to the board of directors.	
1885 On November 7, the last spike is driven on the Canadian Pacific Railway's trans-Canada line in British Columbia's Eagle Pass.	**1885** Louis Riel is hanged on November 16 for his role in the North-West Rebellion of 1885.
1888 Van Horne is promoted to the presidency of the CPR.	
1891 Van Horne begins assembling property on Minister's Island, New Brunswick, on which to build an estate that he will call Covenhoven.	
1894 Van Horne is made an Honorary Knight Commander of the order of St. Michael and St. George.	**1894** The Pullman Strike, a nationwide conflict between labour unions and railways, occurs in the United States. Before it ends, it paralyzes the nation's railway system.

Van Horne and His Times

Canada and the World

1896
Gold deposits are discovered in Bonanza Creek in the Yukon, which sparks the Klondike (Yukon) Gold Rush.

Wilfrid Laurier becomes Canada's seventh prime minister.

1898
While still president of the CPR, Van Horne begins assembling land for a stock farm at East Selkirk, Manitoba.

1899
Van Horne resigns as president of the CPR on June 12. He is kept on as a director, however, and is appointed to the newly created office of board chairman. As chairman he is an *ex officio* member of the CPR's executive committee.

1900
Van Horne founds the Cuba Company to build a trunk railway that will run along Cuba's spine, linking the seaport of Santiago at the island's east end with Havana at the west end.

1901
Queen Victoria of the United Kingdom dies on January 22, 1901, after reigning longer than any other female monarch in history. She is succeeded by her son Edward VII.

Van Horne and His Times | *Canada and the World*

1901
President William McKinley of the United States is assassinated by an anarchist on September 6, 1901. He is succeeded by Theodore Roosevelt.

1902
The last spike is driven on the Cuba Railroad on November 11.

1910
Van Horne resigns from the chairmanship of the CPR.

1911
To harvest and can the sardines of Passamaquoddy Bay, Van Horne establishes the Canadian Sardine Company. He also participates in the election of 1911 as a forceful opponent of reciprocity.

1912
On the night of April 14, the *Titanic*, the largest ship afloat and touted as the safest, strikes an iceberg in the Atlantic Ocean and sinks.

1914
The First World War erupts. When Britain declares war on Germany on August 4, Canada is automatically at war.

1915
In June of this year, Van Horne accepts the chairmanship of a federal commission that will

Van Horne and His Times	*Canada and the World*
examine agriculture, immigration, transportation, the borrowing of capital, and the marketing of food products.	
On September 11, Van Horne dies in the Royal Victoria Hospital in Montreal following surgery for a large abdominal abscess. His funeral takes place on September 14 at the family mansion on Sherbrooke Street West.	

Bibliography

Hart, E.J. *The Selling of Canada: The CPR and the Beginnings of Canadian Tourism*. Banff: Altitude Publishing, 1983.

Knowles, Valerie. *From Telegrapher to Titan: The Life of William C. Van Horne*. Toronto: Dundurn Press, 2004.

Lamb, W. Kaye. *History of the Canadian Pacific Railway*. New York: Macmillan Publishing Ltd., 1977.

Lavallée, Omer. *Van Horne's Road: An Illustrated Account of the Construction and the First Years of Operation of the Canadian Pacific Transcontinental Railway*. Montreal: Railfare Enterprises, 1974.

MacKay, Donald. *The Square Mile: The Merchant Princes of Montreal*. Vancouver: Douglas & McIntyre, 1987.

Martin, Albro. *James J. Hill and the Opening of the Northwest*. New York: Oxford University Press, 1976.

McDonald, Donna. *Lord Strathcona: A Biography of Donald Alexander Smith*. Toronto: Dundurn Press, 1996.

McDowall, Duncan. *Quick to the Frontier: Canada's Royal Bank*. Toronto: McClelland and Stewart, 1993.

McPherson, James. *Battle Cry of Freedom: The Civil War Era*. New York: Oxford University Press, 1988.

Thompson, Norman and Major J.H. Edgar. *Canadian Railway Development from the Earliest Times*. Toronto: The Macmillan Company of Canada Limited, 1933.

Vance, Jr., James E. *The North American Railroad: Its Origin, Evolution, and Geography*. Baltimore: The Johns Hopkins University Press, 1995.

Vaughan, Walter. *The Life and Work of Sir William Van Horne*. New York: The Century Company, 1920.

Index